Cephalonia

Cephalonia
Luigi Ballerini

Translated by Evgenia Matt

RAIL EDITIONS — BROOKLYN, NEW YORK

Published by Rail Editions
253 36th Street, Unit 20, Brooklyn, NY 11232
www.brooklynrail.org

Rail Editions, the publishing wing of the *Brooklyn Rail*, publishes books of art and literary criticism, poetry, experimental fiction, prose meditation, artists' writings, and works in translation.

ISBN-13: 978-0-9907881-3-3

First English Edition, 2016
Translation © Evgenia Matt
First published by Arnoldo Mondadori Editore, Milano, 2005.

Rail Editions is distributed by SPD:
Small Press Distribution, 1341 Seventh Street
Berkeley, CA 94710 | 800.869.7553
orders@spdbooks | www.spdbooks.org

Cover:
Robert Motherwell, *[Untitled (Black Shape)]*, 1975. Acrylic on paper, 26 x 20 1/2 inches (66 x 52.1 cm), irreg. Courtesy of the Dedalus Foundation, © Dedalus Foundation, Inc./Licensed by VAGA, New York, NY.

The author and the translator wish
to express their gratitude for the very
special contributions to the translation
of *Cephalonia* made by Erika Nadir,
Andrew Hiltzik and Tom Sleigh.

CONTENTS

To Paola
who ups the ante

CEFALONIA 1943 – 2001
(MONOLOGO A DUE VOCI)

CEPHALONIA 1943 – 2001
(MONOLOGUE IN TWO VOICES)

Fingebant. . .credebantque
Cornelio Tacito, *Annali* VI, 5.10

Prima se la cuntaven su e poeu ghe credeven
Lo stesso, in dialetto milanese

Fingebant. . .credebantque
Cornelius Tacitus, *Annals* VI, 5.10

Prima se la cuntaven su e poeu ghe credeven
The same, in Milanese dialect

First they made it up and then they believed it

ETTORE B

sulla mia morte non ci sono dubbi. Ne rimangono invece
intorno ai modi: caduto, secondo la vulgata, su di un'arma
quasi bianca, e dopo giorni di attacchi rinviati, insidïosa
corre anche voce che sia stato messo al muro. Non poteva,
l'incertezza, non turbare chi del mio silenzio s'era fatto
una specie di ragione, sia pure a mezzo di sarcasmi e scatti
di non trattenibile violenza (come assente ho suscitato attese
di esperienza che sarei stato fiero di evitare). Sforzandomi
di contare come vivo, ho comunque istigato non illeciti
e non sospetti annusamenti di verità: che una mala fede,
per dirne una, si osservi meglio se un ribrezzo intermittente
soggiace alle lusinghe di un dio massaggiatore, o quando
non gracchia al modo delle rane, né urla s'ode a destra uno
squillo di tromba cui risponde uno squillo, a sinistra. Sapersi
maschere sdipana sintomi di parossismo, di chiaroveggenza
(esserci, starci, cantare per farsela passare, per capire chi ha
chiesto e chi ha pagato impunemente il conto, la zavorra).
Vivi o morti, è da vivi che si tenta di tornare sui passi del
proprio delitto, che ci si torna, untuosi, fingendosi morti

ETTORE B

there's not a shred of doubt that I am dead. There's some
debate as to how it happened: fallen, according to all
reports, in open combat, after days of delayed attacks, some
nasty rumor ran they put me up against the wall. Uncertainty
could not but shake one who had fashioned my silence
into a sort of reason, by means of sarcasm, or surges of
insuppressible wrath. (My absence aroused expectations
I would have been proud to avoid.) Struggling to be counted
with the living, I stirred up unsuspected but not illicit whiffs
of truth: that bad faith, to name one, is better noticed when
an intermittent loathing succumbs to the flatteries of a God-
masseur, or when it doesn't croak like frogs, nor screams,
when to the right you hear a trumpet blast answered by a
blast on the left. Awareness of a masked existence unfolds
unsuspecting symptoms of clairvoyance and paroxysm (to
be in it, to stay with it, singing to feel better, to understand
who, without guilt, asked for and paid the bill, who dumped
the ballast.) Dead or alive, it is as living we retrace the steps
of our crime, and return to it, unctuously, feigning death

HANS D

scrupoli non ho che siano duri e molli come paraffina o come
olio di canfora, o di merluzzo, e diano abbrivio alla rimonta,
al rinnovamento ideale che viene a galla o slitta nel dare avere
di un'afosa teoria di santi e di megere: da ogni punto di vista
il mio è l'esempio più subdolo e inattaccabile, più ostinato e più
affetto da ritrosia. Mio, per capirsi, come "me la tengo stretta"
e "parlo per denegare tracce di connivenza privilegiata, di luce
che avvilisce la penombra del senso". Sono tracce che non c'è
bisogno di seguire fino in fondo: perfino i miei *pro tempore*,
le mie magagne affossate, possiedono la lugubre destrezza
di un esilio dove il filo spinato si confonde coi rami spinosi
di un cordoglio, di una passione imprecisa. Mio, come lo stile
con cui elargisco ceste febbrili di pane bianco. E poiché nulla
si può elargire al di fuori di allarmanti somiglianze, mio come
"vicariamente", o lettera nascosta sotto il naso di tutti, caduti
e fucilati, nei giorni di un settembre che la pioggia non cessò
di picchiare, argentina, sui tegoli del tetto, sul fico e sul moro

HANS D

I have no scruples, firm or soft like paraffin, or camphor
or cod liver oil, scruples that give headway to the comeback,
to the ideal revival surfacing or sliding into the debit and credit
of a sweltering theory of saints and hags: no matter how you
look at it, mine's the most devious and most impervious example,
the most persistent and afflicted by reluctance. Mine, to be sure,
as in "I don't give it up" and "I speak to deny all the traces of
a privileged guile, a light that shames the shadow of sense."
No need to follow these traces to the root: even my *pro tempore*,
my buried flaws, possess the melancholy skill of an exile, a scattered
passion where barbed wire blends with thorny branches of sorrow.
Mine, just like the style of giving away feverish baskets of white
bread. For nothing can be given away except alarming likenesses,
mine like "vicariously", or a letter hidden under everybody's nose,
the fallen and the shot, in those September days when a silvery rain
kept beating, on the roof tiles, on the fig tree, and the mulberry tree

ETTORE B

fronda non direi ma un surrogato di mezza stagione, una pallida ecchimosi adorata in luogo di tremore, di tumore arrogante, o con voglia di scherzare. E neppure doppio gioco, doppio incastro di una volontà che si attiva tuonando parole d'ordine (tracciare con l'aratro il solco, difenderlo con la spada, fare la guardia ai fusti di benzina). Meno che mai martirio per cui si accede, anche non battezzati (che ne basta il desiderio), alla gloria di santi che sapranno intercedere presso la madonna pellegrina, la quale saprà intercedere anche lei presso la divina potestà, modificando gli esiti di una disfatta logica prima di tutto. Teniamoci quindi ai fatti emergenti dalla certezza dell'altrui vacillare, all'inganno pregiato che divide l'intenzione dal suo dichiararsi; e salpiamo solamente a partire da elisioni che schiumano nel brodo di referenti spostati e condensati, cui vanno soggette alcune affabulazioni compensative: "Essere dei nostri" potrebbe voler dire aver trovato Dio che dormiva ed essersi sottratti al suo disdegno, all'invito di decifrare l'emblema del suo distendersi nel mondo per dargli luce. Lasciamo per tanto a chi le merita (per ceto e usanza) le stellette che noi portiamo e le *culottes* che invece non portiamo e sono la fottutissima croce di *noi soldaaa*

ETTORE B

I wouln't say dissent but a mid-season surrogate of it, a pale,
beloved contusion, in lieu of tremor, of an arrogant tumor,
aching to crack a joke. Not even double crossing, the double
joint of a will that awakens, thundering watchwords (to cut
furrows with a plow, defend it with the sword, to keep guard
over gasoline tanks). Still less the martyrdom that leads even
the unbaptized (desire alone will do) to the glory of saints
who can plead with a Madonna who travels door to door and
can plead with the Almighty, altering above all the outcome
of a logical defeat. So let us stick to the facts emerging from
the certainty of someone's wavering, to the prized deceit that
divides an intention from its enunciation; and let us sail from
the elisions foaming in the broth of displaced and condensed
referents affecting several fables of compensation: "To be on
our side" could stand for finding God asleep and fleeing his
contempt, his invitation to decode the emblem of his stretching
over the earth to flash light on it. Let's leave to those who deserve
them (out of class and habit) the little stars we wear and the
culottes we don't, and are the fucking torture *of us soooldiers*

HANS D

non sono di quelli che tirano mattina per dire che la faccia di un Jack
Palance è la prova che dei buoni ce n'era perfino tra i nazi e ce n'è
tuttavia, sontuosamente affrescati con la luger in mano e le bretelle.
Sostengo, questo sì, che per aggiungere "me ne vanto" a "me ne frego"
(e farsi conoscere dallo straniero) non è necessario invocare i vantaggi
di una coerente lungimiranza: basta convincersi di aver vinto una volta
per tutte la tentazione di figurare in prima persona. Chi oserebbe parlare
di *Zeitgeist* per dei rami di pesco che vende al quadrivio una vecchia
«mentre piove e spiove sotto l'aspro alternar delle ventate»? Quand'anche
non avesse un suo figlio mangiato del mio pane azimo, non sarà questa
filologia da rimasto a galla, a tenerlo lontano dai pericoli di una latitante
apoteosi: la lugubre voglia d'incidere nel sociale si ottiene osservando
chi con ciclica disinvoltura si pente di errori commessi illustrando il ritmo
inarrestabile del proprio emanciparsi: regina di cuori è diverso da regina
prematura, da prezzo elevato che non dura, che non può durare, diverso,
per natura, dal disprezzo che amo, da cui debbo astenermi con cura

HANS D

I'm not one who stays up nights and claims the face of Jack Palance
proves there were good men even among the Nazis, as even now
there are, sumptuously frescoed with suspenders and Luger in hand.
But I do maintain that to add "I'm proud of it" to "I don't give a damn"
(and let foreigners know who we are) you need not have the advantage
of a coherent foresight. Quite enough the conviction to have stifled once
and for all the temptation of upmanship. Who would dare call Zeitgeist
the peach blossoms a little old woman sells at the crossroads "while it
rains and pours among bitter gusts of wind"? Even if some child of yours
had not eaten of my unleavened bread, this left-afloat philology would
not spare him the dangers of a fugitive apotheosis. The melancholy wish
to bring about social change comes from observing those who with cyclic
nonchalance repent mistakes illustrating the relentlessly bold rhythm
of their own emancipation: queen of hearts is different from queen
premature, from the high prices that cannot and will not endure, apart
by nature, from the disdain I love, from which, with care, I must forbear

ETTORE B

le tinga dunque un altro le camicie aborrite del regime, le rifaccia *drip and dry*, le affidi a un mercato eccitato, splendidamente rinnovato, assiepato, più dinoccolato di Gary Cooper, più allampanato di Buster Keaton, vittima d'insidia, non di eroico furore. Ma io vago insepolto, elargito a sproposito, e mi è chiara la violenza di un pensiero in linea retta, che si posa sui clivi e sui colli, con arpe d'oro, e riposa su torri atterrate, un pensiero che non sa dirsi: "torna indietro", come carta giocata incautamente, come parola accolta ma non da noi generata, che a ballarci intorno qualcuno ci troverebbe il bandolo di una matassa: non coincidono scatto e comando, scatto e comandamento? Aveva anche il Duce due corni di luce che nessun marmo riproduce? Non era già un obbedire il suo credere, il suo truffare? Oggi è lo stridere di voglie azzerate che induce il dubbio a togliersi di mezzo, a sputtanare il racconto di un'orgiastica reticenza. E non lo sanno forse i paredri, gli economisti squadristi e le ballerine della Scala, che il cuore non è uno strumento scordato, che può cantare quando e dove vuole, o darsi pace, o anche rimediare una sberla, se proprio sbaglia nel dire "fine de la comedìa…"

ETTORE B

let others dye them, the reviled shirts of the regime, let them drip-dry,
entrust them to an excited market, splendidly revived, crowded, more
skin-and-bones than Gary Cooper, lankier than Buster Keaton, victim
of ambush, not heroic frenzy. But wandering, unburied, inauspiciously
given away, I clearly see the violence of rectilinear thinking, alighting
on hills and slopes, with golden harps, nestling among desolate towers;
the kind of thought that cannot say "come back" like a loosely played
card, or like a word we've welcomed, but not generated, a word that,
should we prance around it, might unravel the ball of the yarn. Dart
and command, leap and commandment, do they not crisscross? Didn't
the Duce shine forth two horns of light that no marble could ever reproduce?
Wasn't his own belief, his swindling, the same as his obedience? Today
the screech of emptied yearnings persuades doubt to hit the road, to badmouth
the tale of an orgiastic reticence. Don't the minor gods, the embedded
economists, the ballerinas at La Scala know the heart is not an untuned
instrument, that it can sing both when and where it wishes, or find its peace,
or even earn a slap, if ever it messes up saying: "end of the show..."

HANS D

buttare non buttiamo mai niente, dai tempi di Arminio, né mai ci siamo
potuti rifare delle grottesche astinenze, dei barriti e del passo che dicono
dell'oca, ma più giusto sarebbe dire di Frankenstein (*dai Galli ci separa
il Reno, il Danubio dai Rezi e dai Pannoni, laddove per Sarmati e Daci
basta il reciproco terrore*). Agl'incubi abbiamo preferito le maschere
rappezzate di una seduzione intirizzita, di una caccia senza quartiere
tra le vampe azzurre della ripulsa e i languori del sapersi autorizzati
ad ammirazioni parziali, al godimento di femmine travisate. In questo
ventre attenuato, in questa grolla di lingue univoche ci accoglie, intuisce,
ci immilla, c'inciotola e c'incoltella un assenso spasmodico e perverso:
no one is met in winning; nessuno che riconosca il gusto struggente
di aggiogare lo schiavo all'aratro prima dell'animale da tiro, del motore
a scoppio. Non sono che feccia gli incontrati, i vinti, gli ebeti uccisi dallo
stupore che qualcuno si fosse armato per ammazzare la gente così...

HANS D

throw out, we never throw out anything, since the days of Arminius, nor
were we ever compensated for our ludicrous self-restraint, for the trumpets
and the goose step, as they call it, though it is more like Frankenstein's
(*from the Gauls we are separated by the Rhine, from Rhaetians and Pannonians
by the Danube, while for Sarmatians and Dacians mutual terror is enough*).
To nightmares we much prefer the patched up masks of a shivering seduction,
an all-out chase among the sky-blue flames of rejection and the indolence of
knowing ourselves entitled to partial admiration, to the relishing of misconceived
females. In this attenuated belly, this goblet of explicit tongues, a nod, spasmodic
and perverse, welcomes, intuits, and increases us a thousand fold, and bowls us,
and knifes us: *no one is met in winning*; no one who has ever known the heart-
breaking joy of yoking slave to plow before draft animals and combustion engines.
Nothing but scum are all those we met, the beaten, the half-wits killed by
the disbelief that someone could have taken arms to slaughter people so

ETTORE B

i più non rubano direttamente pur essendo inclini al profitto, alla non
trascurabile analogia di sesso e cucina (battere con cura, umettare, con
una briciola di zucchero togliere eventuali acidità, cuocere tra due
fuochi, servire o caldo o freddo); i più disprezzano senza inviperire
chimere redentive, scollamenti di senso che finirebbero col darglielo
un senso al sapore che invade, inconfondibile, la bocca, nel punto
in cui l'abbandona l'entusiasmo per la strage; e non l'abbandona per
cautela, ma per insolvenza, perché non è reciproco il disprezzo.
(Non è disprezzo il disinganno di camerieri che pompano a dismisura
l'asimmetria delle scalmane, dei *vol-au-vent*, o di alcuni tronchi
dilaniati nel bosco come sacchi di coloniali.) Quanto a voi... come
accogliere l'adorazione di servi perennemente atterriti e burleschi?
Da cui viene che una ragione, quel sapore tedesco e quel disprezzo
tramandato debbono averla avuta, e averla tuttavia. Perché demeritarla,
fingendo che non l'altro in voi, ma altri avesse voluta questa guerra
cui neppure la morte sa mettere fine? che colma i boccali e li svuota
con l'acribia di una supina melanconia, che si stira e si avvolge in lana
superstite, in pagina voltata languidamente? Che con me, oltretutto,
non attacca, perché c'ero, e se c'ero, guardavo, e se anche non guardavo
vedevo, come ancora vedo e m'avvedo che neppure Lei ha mai saputo
dire, sorridendo, "fine de la comedìa". Né ci sono entusiasmi o malori
che bastino ad inquinarla la passerella del suo *café chantant*... erano
biondi biondi biondi i bei capelli corti, alla bebè, erano tondi tondi
tondi i bei gioielli del suo *décolleté*... anche se bevuta d'un fiato
una birra rimane, come dire, un simbolo, un'espressione d'amore

ETTORE B

most do not steal directly, though inclined to profit, to the oh so
fruitful analogy of sex and cooking (beat gently, moisten, reduce
possible acidity with a pinch of sugar, cook in a large Dutch oven,
serve either hot or cold). Without a trace of fury, most disdain
redemptive illusions, the collapsing of senses that would explain
the unmistakable taste filling the mouth when the thrill of the
massacre deserts it... not as precaution, but from insolvency. For
the feeling of disdain could not be reciprocal. (The disenchantment
of waiters blowing out of proportion the asymmetry of excited hot
flashes, or *vol-au-vents*, or tree trunks torn to pieces, like sacks
of groceries in the woods, is not disdain.) As to yourselves... how
to accept the worship of servants perennially terrified and farcical?
Clearly that German flavor, that handed down contempt must have
had a reason, and must have one still. Why degrade it, pretending
that not some Other in you, but others had wanted this war that
death itself cannot end, that fills and empties mugs with the precision
of a supine melancholy, stretched and wrapped in the surviving wool
of an indolently turned page? It takes much more than this to fool me,
for I was there, and if I was, I was watching, and even if I didn't watch,
I saw, as I still do, that not even you, dear sir, have learned to say, with
a smirk, *"end of the show".* No thrill or swoon could ever spoil the
walkway of your precious *café chantant*... ah they were blond, blond,
blond, those little baby bangs, and they were round, round, round
the lovely jewels of her *décolleté*... gulped down, a glass of beer
remains a symbol, if you will, an expression of true love

HANS D

io mi son uno che di tutte le voglie del mondo, tranne quella per cui
mi fingo inquilino di un Olimpo dove oggetti africani fanno a pugni
con maniglie di alluminio e quadri nostrani d'avanguardia, potrei
sbarazzarmi con dovizia di particolari: so ballare, tirare di scherma,
so fare i salti mortali. Ho consentito a mio padre di girare il mondo,
di buscarsi un tozzo di pane e un bicchiere di birra. E al padre di
suo padre, e al padre del padre di suo padre. È da lì che mi viene
il sangue freddo che ci vuole per fare due chiacchiere senza mai
sovvertire, con ondate di entusiasmo, la gergale allegria del rimosso,
per scrivere anch'io di oggetti esagerati la cui trasparente indulgenza
ha fatto di me uno sfuggito a se stesso. Fucilare non è né un giudizio,
né uno sfogo. Vincere, invece, sparando a chi, potendo, ti sparerebbe
è un giudizio. E chi ha investito in vittorie non può tollerare avversari
indegni delle sue prodezze. Ai meno forti Omero non prescrive lepide
frustrazioni, ma quella fetta di fortuna e divino sgomento che abiliti
anche loro a nuocere, a *noscere* senza la esse (o con la *esse* doppia).
È chiaro: squattrinamento vuol dire alibi costante, e io lo vedo, dalla
mia finestra enfatica, come, atterrita, la gente ne approfitti, da morta
e da viva, io che so ballare, tirare di scherma e fare i salti mortali che
consentono a un padre (e al padre di un padre) di girare il mondo
moltiplicando pani di farina bianca e pesci di non riscattabili allergie

HANS D

but for feigning to dwell on a Mount Olympus where African art
clashes with aluminum door handles and paintings of our local
avant-garde, I could ditch all the whims in the world and do it
with a wealth of details: I can dance, and fence, I can turn
somersaults. I gave my father a chance to see the world, earn
a loaf of bread, and a glass of beer. And the father of his father,
and the father of his father's father. That's where I get the cold
blood it takes to chat without jeopardizing, with waves of zeal,
the mirthful jargon of what is missing; or to write about inflated
topics whose see-through indulgence made me a fugitive from
myself. Shooting is not the same as judging, nor does it cause
anyone to blow off steam. To win however, shooting those who
would fire back, if they could, is judgment (investing in victories
implies despising unworthy enemies.) Homer doesn't grant the weak
facetious frustrations, but that portion of luck and divine dismay
that enables them also to do harm, to *noscere* without an S (or with
a double S). It's clear: pennilessness is their perpetual alibi, and I
can see it, from my emphatic post, how the terrified exploit it, dead
or alive. I who can dance, and fence, and somersault, and give
a father (and a father's father) a chance to see the world, to multiply
white flour loaves of bread and fish of unredeemable revulsions

ETTORE B

da vecchio, a un eroe non gli va di grattarsi la schiena contro un tronco
gonfiabile, di palma, comperato all'aeroporto insieme agli armamenti
del *relax* più completo (spugne, vibratori incessanti); per lui la guerra
non finisce con le assi schiodate della sorpresa, con il sottrarsi al vero
di una corrispondenza materiale, né quando l'oscillazione prematura
dell'ascissa lo avverte della nascita di un pensiero, di un consenso
liquido e anticipato, avvolto nella paglia semisommersa di un ascolto:
siamo alle prese con un colmo di rutilante *umheimlich*: non eravate solo
i tedeschi, eravate il destino, disattento o ignaro della prematurità
del pensiero. Impreparati ai frutti dell'incoerenza, i degradanti esempi
che ve ne offriva chi le reni alla Grecia non le aveva nemmeno accarezzate
(più il veleno di un sole garantito), vi convinse che il prezzo dell'infamia
fosse preferibile all'infamia del disprezzo: si può uccidere chi è stato
acquistato, ma i disprezzati non c'è maniera di acquistarli, né, con pudore,
di annientarli. Sarebbe pertanto cosa degna e giusta, equa e salutare che
un Ciampi, rivierasco e pietroso (avvezzo al candore del signore di Pilo,
ma non al tremito incalzante di una Pizia posseduta), la piantasse di fare
'o piezz 'e core, l'equilibrista indignato che salta e balla e tira di scherma
per richiamare il popoltutto all'arengo, per chiedere giustizia postuma
all'odiato nemico (che odiato però non risulta a chi gli compra lamiere
a tutto spiano, e col denaro in mano e che di stragi, oltretutto, dichiara
di averne avute abbastanza). Ahi, quanto a dir sarebbe cosa giusta,
et equa et robustosa et forte, se avvertisse anche lui, sotto gli enormi
piedi, il sussulto del peggio in cui precipita la sua sapienza di custode
non dell'equo (del giusto, e del salutare), ma dello scempio de' lavacri
e dell'are, e perfino del Lingotto di cui nuovamente va fiera la nazione!
Sveglio, a tratti, dalla pennica del suo capitale (del discorso che non

circola, che non si ascolta, che non si avvolge al grissino di un messaggio sprofondato nel corpo emotivo dell'esperienza), non sarebbe, il vindice Ciampi, uomo anche lui del destino, figura figurata che consente di restare aggrappati a un qualche delirio contubernale (ma che bello il bel paese dove il sì suona) e disprezzare un disprezzo che funziona invece come un guanto, come un pennello? E se non il disprezzo, almeno il cavagnuolo della sfiga rintuzzata, il cestello per cui rabbrividisce ogni figliolo, ogni fringuello illegale o rondinotto che aspetti, sospettoso, le sue zanzare

ETTORE B

when he grows old, a hero doesn't care to scratch his back against
inflatable palm trunks, picked up at the airport along with the stock
in trade of total relaxation (sponges, perpetual vibrators). For him war
does not end with the loose planks of surprise, the turning away from
the truth of factual correspondence, nor when the premature oscillation
of an abscissa alerts him that a thought is about to be born, a liquid and
expected consent, wrapped in the barely submerged straw of listening:
we are up against an overdose of dazzling *umheimlich*: you were not
just Germans; you were fate, heedless or unaware of the prematurity
of thought. Unprepared for the fruit of contradiction, the vile examples
offered you by those who couldn't even whip the kidneys of Greece (plus
the poison of a perfect sun), convinced you the price of infamy was
more acceptable than the infamy of disdain: those you buy you can kill,
but you can't buy those you disdain, nor shamelessly annihilate them.
Would it not be *dignum et justum et salutare* if stony and coast-dwelling
Signor Ciampi (accustomed to the candor of Lord of Pylos, but not to
the unremitting tremor of the possessed Pythia) were to quit the *piece
o' my heart* philosophy of an offended tightrope walker who does
somersaults and dances, and fences, to call the whole nation to order
and demand posthumous justice from the hated enemy (hated no longer
by citizens who flat out pay cash in hand for his metal sheet and state,
furthermore, they have had quite enough of massacres). It would be *just and
fair and powerful and wild,* if under those giant feet of his, he could feel
the wisdom of his guardianship fall into the throbbing abyss where not the
aequum (and the *justum*, and the *salutare* are guarded,) but the defilement
of founts and altars, and even of the Lingotto in which the nation takes pride
once again. Sporadically awakened from the catnap of his capital (a corralled

and neglected discourse, not rolled around the breadstick of messages rooted in the emotional body of experience), might it not be that avenging Signor Ciampi, himself another man of destiny, is the *figura figurata* enabling us to cling onto some contubernal frenzy (Oh, how beautiful the lovely land where *sì* resounds…) and show disdain for a disdain that fits like a glove, like a jig-saw-puzzle? And should disdain be not appropriate, at least the warding off of rotten luck, the little basket that makes every young lad shiver, and every outlawed finch or wary fledgling waiting for its mosquitoes

HANS D

poiché siamo in un campo di solchi neri, di zolle ribaltate, remissive,
remote alla più parte dei presunti vivi, e m'assicurano le smorfie
di una qualunque coscienza, confesserò che un antico imbarazzo
accompagna, per la mia gente, l'idea di soluzione: se uno guadagna
e sfrutta il guadagno per guadagnare, inaridisce il godimento in lui
della propria inespugnabile isteria. *Si tolgano, a scanso di sorprese,*
tutti gli organi interni che, avvolti in tele purissime di lino, troveranno
ricetto in canopi alabastrini separati. Replica, in questo caso, rimane
desiderio, e l'occasione si annuncia come povertà di un pensiero
messo in mostra. Né dovremo rimetterci noi sotto coperte impaurite,
protetti da una coerenza cui siamo immuni e assuefatti. È compreso
nell'andirivieni il progetto di un guadagno ulteriore per rimediare
al male prodotto dal guadagno iniziale. Il socialismo… un albero
germogliato al chiuso: potessi mangiarne i frutti per vedere l'effetto
che fanno. E non conta di più aver vinto la guerra, anche avendola
perduta? Perduta dalla *Wehrmacht* ma vinta da *Strangelove* per cui
un'angoscia, nel sogno ricorrente, equivale alla sfida del tradurre:
Graecia capta. Ma chi avrebbe mai concesso, nell'acuto ripullulare
di un abbandono che avevamo pensato tutto nostro, che fosse più ricco
il vostro, e più buio, e più insaziabile: *quis talia fando Mirmidonum*
Dolopumve aut duri miles Ulixi temperet a lacrimis, se avrà davvero
porto orecchi intenti? Fatale, la nostra lotta, fu solo per modo di dire:
Camerati dell'Armata italiana, l'Italia fascista è stata… e la Germania
nazional-socialista è stata dal traditore Badoglio ab…ban…do…na…ta,
ma voi, figli di una stravagante chimera, voi ficcati nella *pietas* di una
disordinata indifferenza, non avevate sintesi e nemmeno uno straccio
di antitesi, che dico, di ipostasi o speranza di pareggio, di goal della
bandiera che desse un lurido senso al massacro, all'odore strinato
del vostro incallito trasformismo, e lo scrisse il generale Hubert Lanz
sui volantini: *Deponete le armi,* quasi si trattasse della *depositio barbae*
di fanciulli togati surrettiziamente: *Noi questa lotta non la vogliamo.*
E aggiunse, per lusingare: *Sarete annientati da forze preponderanti*

HANS D

as long as we are in a field of black furrows, of overturned, meek clods
beyond the reach of the presumed alive, and get some comfort from the
grimaces of an incipient awareness, I will freely confess that for my
people an ancient shame goes hand in hand with the idea of solution:
if you earn money and exploit it to earn more money, the relish of your
own invincible hysteria withers away. *To avoid any surprise, remove*
all internal organs, wrap them in the purest linen cloth and store them
in separate canopy jars. Replicas, here, will linger on as yearnings, while
opportunity will be ushered in like the paucity of a thought put on display.
Nor will we ever need to hide again under a fright of blankets, protected
by a consistency which we have grown familiar with and immune to.
Included in the back and forth is the plan of further gains required to repair
the evil of the initial profit. Socialism… a tree sprouted indoors: if I
could only taste its fruit and learn how it affects us. Doesn't it matter more
to have won the war after losing it? Lost by the *Wehrmacht*, won by *Dr.*
Strangelove, so that angst, in a recurring dream, can match the challenge
of translating *Graecia capta*. Who could imagine, in the keen resurgence
of a neglect we thought all ours, that yours was richer, darker, more
insatiable: *quis talia fando Myrmidonum Dolopumve aut duri miles Ulixi*
temperet a lacrimis if he has truly perked his ears? Our fight was driven
by destiny only in a manner of speaking: *Comrades of the Italian Army,*
Fascist Italy… and Germany, and National Socialist Germany have been
a… ban… doned by the traitor Badoglio. But in you, children of a weird
illusion, thrust into the *pietas* of a wild apathy… no synthesis ever lodged,
nor a shred of antithesis, what am I saying, of hypostasis, no hope for an
even match, not even for a consolation goal that could inject some filthy
sense into the massacre, into the singed odor of your callous turn-coating.
Colonel Hubert Lanz wrote it clearly in the leaflets: *Lay down your arms,*
as if it were a *depositio barbae* for sneaky boys in togas. *We don't want*
this fight. Then added coaxingly: *Superior forces will destroy you all*

ETTORE B

der die das, der die das, i lapis smocc fann i spegasc... ma una pioggia
incolpevole accentua i confini e le sorti mutevoli del misurare, il prurito
bisbetico dell'ingiuria che abbrevia la salmodia, l'inerme ululato della
voglia di erba voglio, del paradigma che sgorga dai tombini come acqua
alta, come perdita ignorata, inzaccherata, non confluita nella partita doppia
delle risposte adeguate: *der die das, der die das, compagn de queji che
fan frecas* per intorbidare la strapazzevole istoria, la parentesi quadra
delle ribellioni intermittenti: era già salda nelle vostre mani urticanti
la palma pretestuosa del campionato, la coppa d'oro che scaccia quella
d'argento, e l'orso amaranto, e l'*ostraneniye* di un'arroganza oftalmica,
turpiloquente, da zona Cesarini... sogna un amore l'estasi dove incarnarsi
e scardina ogni disonestà, ma noi, fuggiasche trappole, irrigidisce un solco
di pura oscenità. Arrotondati e labili, nel bosco che si muove, ci affossa
a più non posso una sgomenta età. Scartabellando ignobili fagotti, lingua
mortal sollecita pellucidi apparati, nottiluche omertà. *Der die das* dei
capitali annacquati, e di quelli esportati, e di quelli espropriati per l'asta,
e di quelli rubati perseverando nelle pratiche domenicali, fuori porta:
pane azimo, sugo di pompelmo... *pancakes*? Scomparti pressurizzati
stagni, inabili allo scoppio, *infin che 'l mar sarà sovra di noi richiuso*

ETTORE B

der die das, der die das, lousy pencils make a mess, alas. . . but a blameless
rain accentuates the boundaries and the erratic fate of measuring, the
nagging itch of curses that cut short the chanting, the defenseless howl
of "wanting never gets", of paradigms gushing out of manholes like high
water, a muddy and neglected loss unrecorded in the ledgers of suitable
responses: *der die das, der die das, and all along the troubled fuss* of
scrambling the mired down threads of history, the square brackets of an
intermittent rebellion. You held already in your stinging hands the pretext
of the championship trophy, the Golden Cup that humbles the Silver, the
Amaranth Bear, the *ostraneniye* of an ophthalmic, and foul-mouthed buzzer-
beating arrogance . . . to turn to flesh love dreams of ecstasy unhinging all
deceit, but we grow stiff, derelict running traps, in furrows of mere lewdness.
Rounded and fleeting in a moving forest we are sunk as deep as ever
by a bewildered age. Rummaging through loathsome bundles, human
tongues elicit diaphanous frameworks, sea-sparkling conspiracies of silence.
Der die das, of inflated capital, exported or expropriated at auctions, and
of the stolen capital persevering in the rites of sunday outings: bread,
unleavened bread, grapefruit juice . . . pancakes? Pressurized, watertight
compartments, impervious to explosion *until the sea would close above us*

HANS D

uno, se gli gira di affermare cose non vere sul proprio conto, c'è il caso
che chi l'ascolta abbia motivi per non dargli torto: ma una tregua senza
rimedio richiede astuzia, laceranti e roride enfiteusi, violenti allacciamenti,
coiti di straforo... chi li avrebbe potuti immaginare diecimila Macbeth da
filodrammatica dell'oratorio capaci, ciascuno per proprio conto, di quello
specialissimo scatto di reni che fa dell'atleta l'eco di un'ombra, di un fumo,
un sospetto imperdonabile di compatimento? non era previsto che fiutaste,
en masse, la pista quieta e smaniosa del delirio per cui prende senso il vivere
dallo stile con cui s'impara, di botto, a dirgli addio. Nell'idea di *surplace*
si contempla la rosa e la cesoia che la decapita, ma per figurarsi le cose come
stanno, per vedervi scritta la propria filigrana simbolica, occorre ostinarsi
a perdere, a darsi per vinti, e senza però arrendersi ai conti che tornano, al
chiaroscuro di una ossessione esuberante, di un ossimoro che spacca in due
la semiosi altalenante della scommessa. A uno, se per dirsi nato di donna,
gli gira di andare a spasso per una città di cubi e di piramidi dolenti, quasi
ci fossero spazi da riscattare, da tradurre in tentazione, a lui che trascura
qualunque istinto di conservazione, si fanno incontro note incoerenti, canti
per gente ignara, zampillante, trascorsa da una gioia che non si ascolta: se
cont ona fetta de gedüld te podet uberwindt quel che te voeuret, se faccia
più impressione un'irrigua e rimandata prateria del vero oppure il vitello
di Aronne, se incalzino ritardi, se uno non è mai del posto e non gli tira

HANS D

if one happens to claim some untrue things about himself, his
listeners may have reasons not to disagree: but a truce with no way
out calls for shrewdness, dewy, earsplitting emphyteuses, violent links,
and coitus on the sly... who could have imagined ten thousand
Macbeths, each one of them capable of that singular back thrust
that turns an athlete into a plume of shadow, of smoke, an unforgivable
hint of insolence? Impossible to predict that, *en masse*, you'd sniff out
the restlessly serene trail of a delirium that causes life to draw meaning
from the style one bids farewell to it? From a track-stand you can draw
the idea of the rose and the shears that behead it, but to see things
as they are, read in them your own symbolic filigree, you must insist
on losing, in giving in without resigning to things as they add up, to
the chiaroscuro of an exuberant obsession, an oxymoron that splits
in half the oscillating semiosis of the wager. If ever, just to feel born
of woman, one gets the itch to strut through a city of sorrowful cubes
and pyramids — as if, neglecting all instincts of survival, there might
still be distances to be redeemed, to translate into temptation — he will
be met by incoherent notes, songs good enough for the unaware, folks
prancing around, run through by clueless and unheeded joys. If with
a slice of *gedüld you can uberwindt* anything you want, if postponed and
well watered prairies of truth, or Aaron's golden calf, leave a deeper mark,
if delays are pressing, and one's never from these parts, and can't get it up

ETTORE B

fa ridere un generale che muore fucilato se morendo urla evviva
il re (che l'ha mollato). Da preferirsi: "Maestà vi porto (e vi lascio)
l'Italia di Vittorio Veneto"? Vittima impegolata nel ruolo di chi
confonde il rischio con l'onore (e lo pensa una specie di duttile
risarcimento, di gelosia retroattiva), l'astuzia, il senso della propria
immodesta recitazione era destinato a sfuggirgli: una vergogna
quel suo commiato messo in atto da una legge che adegua il bene
finale all'esercizio di una coerenza coatta e coibente... aderiamo
al discorso da portare avanti, e indietro, e sulla giostra che ci fa
girare come le stecche di un ombrello, trasaliamo in vista di un
insostenibile lapsus (*e tu biondina...*), che se qualcosa viene a dire
sarà il sospetto che parli di morire, ma senza che qualcuno ne
approfitti, senza che ricada su chi resta il livore dinastico di una
accalorata penitenza (*e tu biondina, capricciosa, garì-baldina,*
al posto di una compromettente *Ave ave... ave Maria*). Si aggiunga
la schiuma di tutte le porte romane con tanto di fanciulle in fiore
che danno la buona sera o il similoro avventizio dei quadrati
costruiti sui cateti. Si consideri il diluvio un buco nell'acqua, una
delega surrettizia, e un cespuglio la sepoltura per chi non giace
in nessun luogo. È nella grafia di queste foibe, nel millantato
credito di questa inscalfibile arenaria che accede alla tragedia
il gregge grigioverde dei saldatori, dei tornitori (*tu sei la stella*),
e dei ringraziati in generale, che per oggi e domani un lavoro
ce l'hanno: e vi accedono, vespe incallite, ricorrendo agli stolidi
sorrisi di chi paga il conto senza guardarlo, perché così è scritto
nel gene dei gaglioffi, dei sarti, dei magliari, dei vagabondi, degli
uscieri tenuti a mollo come dei baccalà, e che sono la spina dorsale
della nazione, della sua ragione (*di noi soldaa?*). Ma se *Dieu* non *lo
vult*, che prezzo avrà la nuova fregatura? Quale sovrumano silenzio
potrà di nuovo abbattersi sul popoloso deserto di un mezzogiorno
qualsiasi, atteso come la manna, disputato da chi ha fretta e da chi

ETTORE B

how laughable, an army general who facing a firing squad cries out "long live the king" (who dumped him). Would he have fared much better with: "Your Majesty, I bring to you (and leave with you) Vittorio Veneto's Italy"? A muddled victim who confuses risk with honor (thinking it must be some sort of pliable reward, a retroactive jealousy), the cunning behind his immodest recitation was bound to escape him. What a shame that farewell, the fatal outcome of the principle equating ultimate good with the practice of a compulsory, insulating consistency... let us stick to the agenda and push forward, and backward, and all around on the carousel that whirls us like the ribs of an umbrella. And let the sight of an untenable slip of the tongue (*sweet little blond...*) catch us off guard, for if there is any meaning to it, it must be that it speaks of death, without profiting from it, however, lest the dynastic lividness of an excited penance falls on those left behind (*my little, fickle blond, my sweet garì baldina... in lieu of a compromising Ave... ave... ave Maria*). Now add the froth of all the *Porte Romane*, complete with young girls in flower, who say Good night and give away the accidental pinchbeck of the squares whose sides are the two legs. Or treat the flood like a hole in the water, a surreptitious proxy; pretend a shrub can mark the burial ground of those who lie nowhere. In the script of these sinkholes, in the pretense of this unscathed sandstone, tragedy welcomes the gray-green flock of welders and carpenters (*you are the star*), and all the grateful men who have work today, and will have it tomorrow. They will be admitted to it, these hardened hornets, resorting to the smiles of those who pay the bills without perusing them, because it is written in the genes of scoundrels, tailors, swindlers, vagabonds and ushers soaked like dried cod: the backbone of the nation, its sole raison d'être (the reason of *us soooldiers?*). But if God does not *vult* it, what will it cost us to be ripped off again? What superhuman silence could hit again the populous desert of an ordinary noon, awaited like manna, disputed by people forever on the run, by all of those who

HANS D

pesa di più la colla (un etto) o un etto di piombo? E del cavallo bianco di Nabulione (da cui smontava per mettere le cose a posto) quale mai sarà stato il colore? Ne nasce una specie di riffa, di timore arruffato, una *pietas* che per dirsi acuta deve badare solamente al proprio idioma, al proprio tornaconto, né mai ripugnare al metallo di una sua indomabile efficacia. Dica lei se un dolore umano irredento (un etto) non pesi più, sulla coscienza, di un etto di vilipesa e stracotta ragione aziendale, o di stato. Anzi non dica niente: per spremere succhi efferati da uno spregevole algoritmo, strizzato fino al punto da fare di una passione un orgoglio, non basta che un tribunale di guerra si affolli di persone subdolamente interposte, a fare da schermo, da segnale, per sostenere che si tratta di "due gocce d'acqua". Ci vuole piuttosto un fardello, una palla al piede, una scuola per sub-normali, o almeno un ritornello, recitabile a ritroso, la croce cucita sul petto di una controfigura, di uno al di sopra di ogni pentimento. Se il regno dei cieli, oggi, è sulla terra e persiste l'idea dei poveri di spirito, non dovrà dirsi l'America quel regno, e non ne stanno i Forrest Gump ereditando gli effetti speciali, il salvacondotto dell'uguale, alla cui legge repelle soltanto il coraggio del *boom-box*, del finocchio venuto al mondo per dissanguare il sistema riproduttivo? Dica lei se questo abuso di condanne, di consensi arruolati, se questo stupro dello sguardo collettivo (del possibile intelletto) cui nullo amato, è chiaro, amar perdona, cui non rincresce remora o dileggio, dica lei se non nasce dal sorriso dolcissimo di un padre a cavallo seguito, sul campo di battaglia, dall'ussaro più amato, intesi entrambi ad atti generosi e stronzi, come il dare da bere agli assetati, il sopportare alcune persone moleste che, mezze morte, ti dicono "caramba" e ti sparano addosso? Anzi non dica niente, che potremmo trovarci anche noi due su quel campo, lei senza senso e foggia, e talmente digiuno di sarcasmi che di più non si può neppure col candeggio, io così affine, sfruculiato, così teratologo in calore, che di più non si può neppure col candeggio

HANS D

does glue (a quarter pound) weigh more, or does a quarter pound of lead?
What might have been the color of Napoleon's white horse (from which
he would dismount to put his things in order)? Something like a raffle
peels off from such dilemmas, a ruffled bashfulness, a *pietas* that to be called
acute must pay attention to its own idiom, its own advantage, and never repel
the metal of its untamable efficiency. You tell me if unredeemed human suffering
(a quarter pound) weighs more than a quarter pound of vilified and overcooked
reason of state (or corporation). On second thought, don't say anything: to squeeze
malevolent juices from a putrid and shrunken algorithm whereby passion turns
into pride, it takes much more than a war tribunal crowded with surreptitious
people, interposed to act like screens or signals, to maintain that passion and
pride are "two peas in a pod". What might work is a bundle, a stumbling-block,
a school for sub-normals, or at least a roundel that can be recited backwards,
the cross sewn on the chest of a stand-in, someone beyond repentance. If the
kingdom of heaven is on earth, and the notion of the poor in spirit is as pervasive
as ever, can't America rightfully be called that kingdom, and aren't all Forrest
Gumps heirs to its special effects, to the safe-conduct of "it's all the same," an
equality whose laws may be repelled only by the courage of boom boxes, or
by queers born to jam the reproductive system? You tell me whether this abuse
of convictions and conscripted consent, this rape of the collective view (of the
possible intellect) that clearly absolves no one beloved from loving back, and
is not affected by either hindrance or mocking, is not born of the sweetest smile
of a father on horseback riding through the battlefield in the company of his
faithful hussar, both of them bent on generous and imbecile acts? To feed
the hungry, quench the thirst of the thirsty and bear patiently the torture
of obnoxious people who, half dead, may rise to say "caramba" and shoot
at you. Actually, do not say anything, for we too might find ourselves out
in that field, you without meaning or shape, so deprived of sarcasm that more
you could not be even with bleach, and I, so self absorbed and taunted, so much
like a teratologist in heat, that more I could not be not even with bleach

ETTORE B

l'idea di consultare i cappellani anziché ordinare un chiaro,
distinto et immediato attacco contro l'ex-alleato rivela, nel
pensiero del comandante, una cospicua componente magico-
religiosa. Quella di rovinare le postazioni, per indurre il
neo-nemico a miti consigli, consente di toccare con mano
l'ambiguità che aggroviglia, nella storia del mondo, soggetto
precario e referente. Fortuna che il *tragos* non poteva farci caso,
perché assorbe in sé ogni mossa e la devolve a inattendibili fini.
Chi sarà? Chi sarà che verrà per dire: ma pensa, ma si può?
Chi chiederà se non sia troppo stretta una Lombardia (da lungi
risonante), la cui pelle ha l'odore del rimpianto, del rialzo dei
prezzi e dei ribrezzi, della doppia causale di versamento?
A chi gioverà la paludosa furbizia di quelli che si sentono
organizzati e tedeschi, solleciti a dire torni presto, cambi,
al massimo, una virgola, o due, e rida, rida per adeguarsi
agli scopi, alle macabre circostanze di una vendemmia
umana senza ripensamenti. Antiquata l'idea dei ponti d'oro,
dell'idiota che può fungere da fungo e poi scapicollarsi
giù da un colle in cerca di rinforzi (a costo, di rimetterci
una gamba, o due); aperto indizio di come fosse già
morto (e liquefatto) chi alle prime, intrattabili luci dell'alba,
si era messo a studiare, con sussiego, le mosse dell'avversario

ETTORE B

seeking the chaplains' advice rather than ordering a clear,
distinct, and immediate attack against the former ally, betrays
the presence, in the commander's mind, of a conspicuous
magic-religious component. Relinquishing strategic positions
to talk the neo-enemy into backing off from the aggression, puts
the finger on the ambiguity entangling, in the history of this world,
the precarious subject and its referents. Our luck that *tragos*
pays no attention to it, for it absorbs and molds each move
into an unreliable purpose. Who will it be? Who will come to say:
just think, how is it possible? Who will deem too narrow the ways
of a Lombardy (resounding from afar), its skin smelling of regret,
the rising costs of repugnance, and the twice repeated motive of
payment? Who will benefit from the marshy shrewdness of those
who feel all organized and German, and quick to say, come back
soon, take out a comma, maybe two, and laugh, laugh without
a second thought, to match the ghastly circumstances of a human
harvest. Outdated, the idea of golden bridges, of idiots who could
fill in for a fungus, then barrel down a hill in search of reinforcements
(at the risk of losing a leg, or even two). A glaring sign that he was
dead already (and liquified) when at the break of an intractable dawn
he haughtily began to study the movements of his adversary

HANS D

incominciando con le raffiche di un mondo alla rovescia, con le barbe
dei cappuccini (da cui le scope per gli spazzini), o con la pelle dei
monsignori (da cui le scarpe per i lavoratori delle piccole e medie
imprese). Non suscita in me che un leggero disappunto la favola dei
talenti raddoppiati e triplicati senza dire come, ma col sospetto che
non si possa se non a prezzo di stupro. E quell'altra secondo cui chi
ti concia per le feste o protegge i propri artigli, il proprio cannone di
felpa e di arguzie, lo fa per il bene di tutti, per dare un esempio. Farvi
fuori (e dentro e sopra e sotto) fu come mollare gli ormeggi allungando
il collo per fingere di rimanere a terra e scuotersi la polvere di dosso

HANS D

beginning with the blasts of a world turned upside down, and Capuchins' beards made into brooms for street-sweepers, and monsignors' skins made into shoes for the workers of small and medium size firms, I feel but the slightest disappointment in the parable of talents, doubled and tripled and multiplied without telling how, though I suspect it can only be done at the price of ravaging. And in that other fable where beating one to a pulp or protecting one's own talons and cannons, even when made of plush and wit, is said to be done for the good of all, to set a definitive example. Finishing you off (and over and under and sideways) was the same as letting go of the moorings, neck stretched out, dust shaken off, pretending to be still on land

ETTORE B

o incominciando con donne che latrate di dolore, che indossate le brache rosse di un debito d'amore, e continuando con singhiozzi da cui traspare una ricerca di stile tirata con i denti: do re mi, mi re do... Se raspando nel cuore stravede (o straparla) il debito che cresce, la sua virtù "a quell'ora" ripopola una voglia di salti, di saltare addosso a qualcuno per mostrargli l'inconsistenza delle sue conclusioni e del proprio vantaggio. Bello o brutto che sia, non è che un ascolto, un facchinaggio da rompersi l'osso del collo

ETTORE B

or else beginning with women and their howls of sorrow, and the red knickers of
their debt of love, and then proceed with the sobbing revelation of a quest
for style pulled by the teeth: do re mi, mi re do… if ever growing debts rasp
in your heart and see what isn't there (or talk of nonsense), its virtue, at that
hour, repopulates a yearning to leap, to jump on someone, throwing at
him the inconsistency of his conclusions, of his advantage. Good or bad as it
may be, listening is all it takes, a dreadful drudgery that will break your neck

HANS D

se coscienza sopita dal consenso, da piena e solidale avvertenza,
rivelasse colpa grave o deleteria, se gettasse vituperio sui modi
precipui dell'acquisto, morirebbe anche in noi la voglia di non
sapere degli ultimi di noi, di volgere in tenebra e silenzio il *fou-rire*
che succede all'incanto del rinascere per forza. Se fosse nudo il re,
il suggeritore, il nato per supporre di sapere, se fosse l'idiota di turno
l'erede del programma in cui concrescono debito e capitale, verrebbe
a noi pure il sospetto che padri e madri sopraggiunti con la piena dei
canali e vaghi di oltranzismo, nulla potessero davanti all'urto di una
somiglianza redentiva che regge le sorti dell'uomo (e della donna,
di lui più evasiva e sparsa, e feudo più smembrato). *Stendere per terra
un tappeto, metterci sopra un seggiola e sedersi. Agitarsi, insoddisfatti,
rizzarsi, tastare, tentennare, riflettere e infine calzare la seggiola con
un biglietto da visita sotto una delle quattro gambe. Rimettersi seduti
e iniziare a dondolarsi. Dondolarsi sempre più forte fino a cascare
a gambe levate.* È il requisito che manca, non la sua requisitoria,
l'incubo che a egregie cose il forte animo accendano l'urne de' forti

HANS D

should grave or detrimental guilt emerge from a mind sedated by full
awareness and deliberate consent, and should that mind revile the ways
by which knowledge is acquired, we too would lose the willpower to learn
about the last of our men and turn to darkness and silence the *fou-rire*
erupting from the surprise of being forced to be born again. If the emperor
has no clothes, and neither does the prompter, the man born from a pre-
supposition of knowledge, if the idiot of the day were to inherit the program
wherein debt and capital are growing side by side, we too would suspect
that fathers and mothers pushed forward by the flooding of the canals,
and charmed by intransigent thoughts, are powerless before the impact
of a redemptive resemblance, ruling over the fate of men (and of women,
more evasive and scattered than men, fiefs more divided). *Lay a rug on the*
floor. Place a chair on it and sit down. Fidget, restlessly, stand up, test it,
ponder, and wedge at last a calling card under one of the legs. Sit down
again and begin to rock. Rock more and more forcefully until you fall over,
feet up in the air. It is the requisite that is lacking, not the requisition,
the nightmare that the urns of the brave may set some noble souls on fire

ETTORE B

al sole si respira, questo è un fatto, e sono i fatti che danno
senso alle cose, che spingono a dirle prima che a qualcuno
venga in mente di schedarle, di addormentarne l'angoscia
e tradurne in orizzonti più vicini, più adesivi, la sfida che
ne promana, che sgrana e non ingrana, la legge fuorisacco,
la tregua del loro smarrirsi. Si può dire: "Siamo e saremo
animali di successo, pechinesi dagli occhi di saccarina"
e non morire mai; oppure *You disappoint me, Mr Bond*
e finire morti con la propria fortuna (sfacciata) alle spalle:
in un campo mezzo grigio e mezzo nero ci sono papaveri
e mammalucchi; mammaliturchi e mammole; ci sono anche
papere d'ingegno che l'affittano a metà con i dindi, che però
non ci sono, stante che per arrivarci bisogna attraversare
un fosso. È irriverente? Non è di sinistra? O è santo, santo,
tre volte santo, il tempo in cui, fischiando il vento (soffiando)
e tuonando la bufera (nevicando la frasca), anche per noi
si tacerà degli ultimi di noi, vedendo inscritta nell'idea
di modello la scomparsa dell'idea di festa? Non sono mai
stato di quelli che godono dell'altrui male (ma irritarmi,
mi irrita assai), e davanti a una strage di fanti che tacciono
per andare avanti, dico che perduto è quello che la spunta,
che si sfrega le mani per farne uscire l'odore della morte

ETTORE B

in the sun you can breathe, that is a fact, and it is facts
that give meaning to things, urging us to speak of them
before someone thinks of keeping a file on them, to put
their anguish to sleep, and turn into a closer, more adhesive
horizon the challenges they issue, that thresh but don't
mesh the law of special delivery, the fair truce of their
perdition. You might say: "We are, and will be, animals
of success, pekinese dogs with sugary eyes" and never die.
Or: "You disappoint me Mr. Bond" and end up dead by
the unheeded sign of an outrageous fortune: the half gray,
half black meadow is full of mamelukes, mammatheturks,
and mammamias, as well as industrious ducklings that
rent it in partnership with turkeys, who are not there, however,
since to get to it you have to cross a ditch. Is it irreverent?
Is this no leftist talk? Or is it holy, holy, holy, the time when
under the whistling wind and the snowing branches, we too
won't talk about the last of our men, seeing the idea of revel
flounder in the idea of pattern? I've never been one to rejoice
in the misfortune of others (it even riles me, at times), but
when I witness a massacre of infantrymen "who silently
march forward" I say that it is the winner who has lost,
who rubs the back of his hands to release the smell of death

HANS D

fortunato al gioco, in amore, coi libri che ho letto e non ho letto,
non sto qui a sifolare l'Aida giorno e notte. Il problema è che una
Deutschland über *alles* sorride, implacata e vile, nel volto idiota
del presidente texano, con abito medio, macchina e moglie medie.
Nessuno è più libero di non strafare, nessuno che abbia diritto
di sapere come andrebbe a finire se amore fosse amare per forza
chi ci ama o ci guarda da sotto in su per ricordarci chi è che comanda.
Non è peccato, no, per carità, non è peccato, ma giocare per vincere,
sapendo di avere già perduto, questo, mi dispiace, non era nei patti

HANS D

lucky at cards, in love, with books that I have and have not read, I'm not here to whistle Dixie day and night. The problem is that a *Deutschland* über *alles* smiles, relentless and vile, on the Texan president's idiotic face, with his average suit, average car, and average wife. No one is free any longer to restrain from exaggerating, no one who has the right to know how it would end if love meant being forced to love back those who love us, or look us over top to bottom to remind us who is in charge. It's not a sin, good gracious, no, not a sin, but playing to win, knowing that you had already lost, I am sorry, that wasn't part of the deal

ETTORE B

a passo di lumaca, di formica, di leone, di gambero (due da leone,
tre da gambero), a passo d'uomo (l'uomo è la misura d'ogni cosa),
anche un *ciolla* può fiutare nel vento l'autunno che porta i quattrini,
le tasse, i corpi dilaniati dalle tasse, e credere in perfetta buona fede
a quel che dice, crederci con l'innocenza, la sicurezza dei *ciolla*.
Non sono i *ciolla* che hanno in mano la legge del calcio, del mio
camino è stretto, del calcinculo? È chiaro che hanno il fiato grosso,
che c'è inerzia in questo mondo così tondo, così spregiudicato che
di più non si può neppure col gorgheggio: *e le giberne che portiamo*
son diiisciplina, son diiisciplina... Queste parole di colore oscuro
vid'io scollate in cima ad un portale, per cui: «maestro» dissi
«saranno buone forse a carnevale, per assolvere i *ciolla* e scorticarne
la razza con mille smanie precluse». «A passi tardi, ma vivaci e loschi,
io nel nome di un padre ti battezzo (per trasferito amore, biascicante,
che, biascicando, spiuma e sgarra), e ti confermo» rispos'egli con lena
affannata, «nel nome di una regola illusoria: a passo d'orso della selva
nera, dell'asino che legge, o con la muta intransigenza dei vampiri.»

ETTORE B

at a snail's pace, at an ant's, a lion's, a crayfish's (two lion's steps, and two crayfish's steps), at a man's pace (man is the measure of all things), even a *chooch* can smell the autumn wind carrying the money, the taxes, the bodies torn to shreds by taxes, believing, in perfectly good faith, in what he says, beaming with candor, bathed in the certainty only a *chooch* possesses. And is it not the *chooches*, who hold sway over the law of soccer, of the chair swing ride, and even of "how tight my chimney ought to be?" Clearly they're gasping for air in this world so exactly lackadaisical and round, so open-minded that it couldn't be more open, not even with a trill in the voice: *the cartridge-pouch we carry, t'is discipliiiine, t'is discipliiiine...* These words in somber color I beheld, hanging from a dark portal, whence I said: "they might be good at Mardi Gras, dear Master, to absolve the *chooches* and flay their ilk with many stifled cravings." "With slow yet brisk and shady steps, I do baptize you in the name of a father (by way of relocated love, a mumbled love that mumbling plucks and errs), and I confirm you" he tiredly replied and out of breath, "in the name of a deceptive rule: at the pace of a Black Forest bear, of someone reading from a wall, 'reader's an ass,' or with the unshakable silence of vampires."

CORO

noi siam li tristi sgarbi accalorati, le formicuzze,
il forellin dolente, noi siam le tristi penne scalcagnate
ch'abbiam copiato quel che voi scrivete, noi siam
le tristi penne imminchionite, e a dire il vero neanche
ben pagate, ch'abbiamo finto quel che voi smentite.
Noi siam queste bellezze sderenate, queste orrende
soffiate malpartite, noi siam queste ideuzze scavalcate
per cui da un po' si azzuffano le fate. Or vi diciàn
perché noi siam partite, avviticchiate dolorosamente,
da quelle mezze strade malfamate dov'eravamo penne
travestite e siamci poste sì presso a la morte ch'altro
di noi non resta che sconcezze in tutt'altre faccende

CHORUS

we're sadly heated bags of rudeness, little ants,
the woeful pinpricks, the slipshod quills that have
transcribed what you have written. We are the sad,
the dumb, and, truth be told, the poorly compensated
quills that feigned the tales you contradicted. We're
the crooked beauties, some sick and badly parcelled
squeals, the obsolete ideas about which fairies have,
of late, begun to squabble. And we shall tell you now
why we have left behind, painfully twined and twisted,
those ill-famed half streets where we were quills
disguised, and have come so close to death that nothing
is left of us, save for some lewd and unrelated matter

HANS D

con la faccia da scemo, il cuore da impaurito, l'anima spaccata in due
da un rigore che non c'era, da una storia di lacrime sul volto di colei
che ha distrutto tutti i sogni miei (esco la mattina presto, torno molto
tardi), in macchina, in bicicletta (sul treno della *IG Farben*) calpesto
avidamente i risultati da cui derivo, conto sulle dita i giorni rimasti,
poi quelli rimasti indietro, voltàti, caduti tutti insieme nel buco nero,
nerissimo delle angherie, nel vigile scottadito di chi si basta, per oggi,
e per domani si peggiora urlando *Montjoie, Montjoie*, fino al midollo,
fino a quando non gli verrà imposto nuovamente di camminare giù
dal marciapiede (fascista? antifascista? *philosophe* che se la mena?),
sussurrando *fiat veritas pereat vita*, ruminando foglie secche, pallottole
di carta da sputare, bevendo un latte nero, nerissimo per fare della storia
una scienza. E qui è la sfida: la sprezzatura di chi uccide, da un lato,
perché sia robusto il domani; dall'altro l'imbarazzo, la convulsione
di chi gioca per ammorbidire, per stendere al sole la trama del presente
quel tanto che basta per infilarci gli spettri inturgiditi da una querula
e nuda lontananza. Se è vero quello che dicono, e sarà vero di certo
se è il vostro comando supremo che lo dice, troverete ogni adespota
fessura spalancata, e non mai abbastanza però quella che accoglie
corpi estranei per ordinarli, e onorarli con polvere d'oro, sapendo
che tutti sono in lotta tra di loro. *(In caso di recapito mancato, re-*
spingere al mittente: dire Acqui è lo stesso che dire Acquisgrana?)

HANS D

with a dope's face, a coward's heart, a soul cut in half by a penalty
kick there was no reason to call, by a story of tears on her face, who
shattered all my dreams (I go out very early and get home late) by
bicycle or by car (on the *IG Farben* train), I trample with a relish on
the results that made me who I am, and count on my fingers the days
that are left, that have been left behind, turned over, fallen altogether
into the black, the blackest hole of vexations, into the piping hot
vigilance of those who now have enough, and later will degenerate,
screaming to the bone *Montjoie, Montjoie,* until they're forced again
to walk along the curb (Fascists, Antifascists, jacking off *Philosophes?*),
whispering *fiat veritas pereat vita,* chewing on a cud of dry leaves and
paper spitballs, drinking the blackest milk, to turn history into a science.
And here's the challenge, the *sprezzatura* of one who kills to strenghten
the days to come, or the embarrassment, the playful convulsion that
softens the day's weft and lays it out in the sun just long enough to slip
in the turgid ghosts of a raw and querulous distance. If it is true what
they say (and it must be true, if it is your High Command that says it),
you will find every orphan crevice wide open, yet none wide enough
to welcome the bodies of strangers, each according to their rank, and
honor them with a sprinkling of golden dust, knowing that they'll all
be fighting one another. (*If undelivered, return to sender. And further-
more: saying Acqui, is it the same as saying Acquis-Granum?*)

ETTORE B

"qui lo dico e qui lo nego" e, per concludere, "spalmami, ma bene, dove non arrivo." (Saltò giù dal tram ma gli furono subito addosso e gli fecero sputare i denti; a quell'altro gli spararono proprio sotto le finestre della scuola, e mandarono tutti a casa.) È lo stesso che dire "l'ho visto e non l'ho visto". Significa che il secondo posto nessuno ce lo toglie, che c'è una pausa nel corto circuito dell'obbedienza, nel dissesto armonico della sequenza. (Ora il Quindici tira diritto fino a Ronchetto delle rane, ben oltre la centrale che le bombe non l'hanno nemmeno sfiorata... colpirono la *ca' de la paura* che sorgeva, e sorge tuttavia, tra rogge mefitiche in località Campazzo.) Più in alto, ecco lì è perfetto; il mare è traditore, se non ti spalmi ti vengono le piaghe

ETTORE B

"here I'll say it, there I'll deny it", and to conclude, "just give me a hand with my sunscreen, nicely, yes, there, where I cannot reach". (He jumped off the trolley, but they were right on him and knocked his teeth out; the other they shot right under our school windows, and sent everyone home.) It is the same as saying "I saw it, but I didn't see it" meaning that none can take second place away from us, that an interruption has occurred in the circuit of obedience, in the harmonious upheaval of the sequence. (These days line 15 goes all the way to *Ronchetto delle rane*, way past the power station that air raids did not even touch... instead they hit *Ca' de la paura* that rose, as it still does, not far from the *Campazzo* amongst the foulest ditches. Higher, higher, there, the sea can be treacherous... if you don't rub it well, blisters are guaranteed

HANS D

al corpo esasperato che dice voglio esserci si oppone
il *trickster* che si presenta sotto forma di animale
(volpe, coyote, coniglio, ragno) e mette a repentaglio
l'idea di verità, sia quella cui si giunge per astrazione,
sia quella che dio non può cambiare, sia quella, infine,
che ognuno si fabbrica temendo la propria castrazione:
un dio che inganni è raro, assai meno un dio protettore
degl'inganni (Ermes, Atena e Loki, tra i vichinghi,
che si oppone agli dei): *milan milan vaffanculo, milan*
inter vaffaonbagn, roma lazio vaffaonbagn. Lo disse
anche Bettino Craxi, e il «Times» di New York tradusse,
stupito, «... told them to take a bath». Noi stessi per
sentito dire cademmo nella logica ventosa di cronache
irredente, delle dispense, dei colpi di spugna, ignari al
cento per cento della madornale lussuria che distingue
l'inferno dall'utopia. Cari amici sportivi in ascolto,
è successo un fatto strano: c'è Badoglio con gli occhiali
che tormenta i generali, che ti ride sulla faccia: l'armistizio
è carta straccia. E poi ci sono le pive nel sacco
di cui non ha equivalente nessuna lingua forestiera.
Neppure in cinese puntiglio fa rima col cartiglio con su
scritto *no pasaran*, ma lì almeno è chiaro che pensare
non vuol dire perdersi tra stoppie sconvolte da un dio
che colpisce da lontano, bensì perdersi senza rimedio
nella risaia, sconfitti dal cuore famelico che la sovrasta

HANS D

the exasperated body that says I want to be there is
opposed by the trickster who shows up under the guise
of an animal (fox, coyote, rabbit, spider) and jeopardizes
both the idea of truth reached through abstraction, and that
which not even god can modify, not to mention the truth
that, fearing castration, each of us fabricates: a cheating
god is rare, less so a god protecting cheaters (Hermes,
Athena, Loki, for the Vikings, who antagonizes other
gods): *milan milan vaffanculo, inter milan vaffaonbagn,*
lazio roma vaffaonbagn. Even Bettino Craxi blurted it out
and the bewildered newsman from the *New York Times*
translated: "told them to take a bath". We too, induced by
 hearsay, fell for the airy logic of unredeemed chronicles,
of lecture notes and slates wiped clean, utterly unaware of
the vastly exaggerated lust separating hell from utopia. Dear
sports fans, stay tuned. Something odd is going on: Four-
eyed Pietro Badoglio is harrowing his own soldiers, and
laughs in their face, gentlemen, this truce is not worth the
paper it is written on. We shall then consider the locution
pive nel sacco whose essence no foreign tongue can capture.
Not even in China a roll of dice can rhyme with a scroll that
reads *No pasaran*, but there, at least, thinking does not mean
being left in a field of stubble ravaged by gods who strike from
afar, but rather hopelessly losing oneself in an arabesque of
rice paddies, defeated by the famished heart hanging over them

ETTORE B

né di mostri si parla impunemente, né gli dei sorridono
a chi di suo ci vede poco e non guida disinvolto. Per farsi
coinvolgere – recita una voce invelenita – c'è più tempo
che vita, e dove tutto è lascia o raddoppia, o quietanza
o traccia inerbita di discorso, può un modello incongruo
scagionarci dall'ubbidire, dal precipitare dalla padella dei
resoconti giulivi nella brace dei sintomi? Anche chi urla
ma se c'ero, se m'hanno visto alla televisione, è libero
di perlustrarsi, di dare del perverso a chi, per mestiere,
accenna a denudarsi. (Lascia perdere che sono i clienti,
oggigiorno, e non quei tirapiedi dei pazienti, che danno
un senso disperato all'idea di diagnosi, all'umiliazione
di un acquisto che amalgama tutti nel sodalizio punitivo
di un capitale detto storia: tutti in marcia verso il mare,
con la risipola e il rubamazzo nella testa, verso un niente
che tira più di una coppia di buoi.) È più mostro chi non
si mostra o chi fa di una sola partita un campionato, una
morte istantanea? E c'è critica o, tutt'al più, c'è rifiuto
nella scelta di un racemo di uva spina, di un'epifania
che schizza in avanti alla ricerca del proprio movente?
Che l'incongruo, se riscalda (a una cert'ora fa perfino
troppo caldo), se fa buon sangue e commuove, alla lunga
non è deplorevole che nasca da una riga, dal rigagnolo
sbilenco e risentito di un inganno. Vince chi s'inganna
di più e meno si dispera, e non guasta che a dare il ritmo
sia la paura ignobile di lettere imbucate per scommessa

ETTORE B

neither you can't, with impunity, speak about monsters nor
do gods smile on those who are short-sighted and drive poorly.
To get involved – a vitriolic voice declares – you have all the
time in the world. And in a world where all is double or nothing,
receipt or grassy trace of discourse, can an unsuitable model
vindicate us from obedience, from jumping out of the frying
pan of gleeful accounts into the fire of symptoms? Even those
who yell "I was there, they saw me on TV", are free to survey
themselves, and label as perverse those who by trade hint at
undressing. (Never mind that nowadays it is the client, and not
the flunky patient who tinges with dejection the idea of diagnosis,
the shame of acquiring that welds us all into a punitive society,
a capital named history: everybody marching toward the sea,
sick with St. Anthony's fire, and a card game of War on their
mind, marching toward a nothingness that pulls harder than
a pair of oxen.) And who are the true monsters, those who
never show, or those who squeeze the whole championship
into a single match, a sudden death? And is there criticism
or mere rejection in the choice of a sprig of gooseberry, of
an epiphany darting out in search of its own motive? When
the unsuitable warms up (and it gets too hot, sometimes), and
puts hair on your chest, or moves you to tears, does anyone
complain if it burgeons out of a single line, a twisted, resentful
rill of deceit? Those who fool themselves the most, and despair
the least, win out in the end, and no harm done if the rhythm
surges from the wretched fear of letters mailed on a bet

HANS D

un campo qualunque va bene, meno quello a fianco dell'alzaia,
col pallone che finisce nel Naviglio e le partite che durano
giornate. È uno scempio per la psiche umana dispendiosa,
dispettosa, aleatoria, che nega che si possa negare e farla
franca. A chi torna gli viene naturale di credersi al centro
di un teatro di salti mortali davanti ai quali impallidiscono
le cerimonie del punto di vista, o dell'indagine: è come un
vaccino, una miccia minima di lebbra, per tenerne in vita
le insinuazioni, la carie del *do ut des*. Non fu per ragionata
e lunga e demiurgica iattura che segnammo noi per primi,
abbandonati dal sublime *Bad dog leo*, ma per colmare con
abilità e rancore un vuoto paronomastico: per tendere l'arco
delle promesse sulla corda verace delle premesse, per insistervi
quasi si trattasse di lettere sfuse in cerca di obiettivo. (Come
neve al sole scomparve anche l'arbitro cornuto, richiamato
ai ruoli d'origine da un silenzio che non ammetteva, e tuttavia
non ammette, ripensamenti.) Fu galeotto il vantaggio ma durò
lo spazio di un mattino. E quelli che hanno l'alibi, o sono
quasi sempre via, o vivono all'ombra di una legge che magari
autorizza, ma non può legittimare, ce l'avranno la voglia
di affermare come in quel tempo di vagoni per "cavalli otto
e uomini quaranta" si contassero (e anche adesso si possono
contare) al posto dei *goals*, le negligenze più colpevoli, i più
laceranti disinganni? Che se la *Champions' League* non c'era,
c'era l'idea del nemico e della barriera e, del pallone, di farne
una bandiera, uno specchio sordido (una preghiera, un puzzo,
un lazzo, una *ruera*) e di abbattere con una sola e fottutissima
cadenza d'inganno (più le amare oscillazioni del suo valore
di scambio) il cardine sciamanico della lusinga (e della paga)
intera. Dell'idillio e della scienza esatta del paradosso, i primi
a rallegrarsi furono gli addetti alla ripetizione, i lunatici fissati
con il catasto, col buon umore, gli osceni del tutto esaurito

HANS D

any field will do except the field running along the towpath —
balls falling in the *Naviglio*, matches going on for days — a
curse for the splurging, mischievous, aleatory human psyche
that denies you can deny things and get away with it. It's only
natural that those who made it back believed to have played
center stage in a theater all somersaults, compared to which
the rituals of perspective and investigation paled like a vaccine,
the smallest fuse of leprosy, sustaining insinuations, like the
decay of *do ut des*. Abandoned by the sublime *Bad dog leo*,
we were the first to score, not out of long, deliberate, demiurgic
desolation, but to fill up, skillfully, with rancor, a paronomastic
void (stretching the chord of premises to bend the bow of true
promises), to insist on it, as if it were a question of a loose
alphabet searching for a target. (The bloody ref melted like
snow in the sun, recalled to his erstwhile role by a silence
prohibiting second thoughts.) Galehaut was the name of our
advantage, but it was gone in the blink of an eye. And won't
those who have an alibi, or are almost never there, or live in
the shadow of a law that may authorize but not legitimize,
won't they wish to affirm that in those days of freight cars
for "eight horses and forty men" scores were kept (as they are
today) not by counting goals but the most irresponsible bursts
of negligence, the most heartrending disillusions? There was
no *Champions' League*, of course, but the notion of "enemy"
was clear, and that of the barrier that might hinder his progress,
or the need to score at least once to save the national honor
(a sordid mirror, a prayer, a reek, a jest, a heap of garbage), and
of knocking down with a single deceptive device, plus the bitter
oscillations of its exchange value, the shamanistic pivot of flattery
and full pay. The first to rejoice at the idyll, at the exact science
of paradox, were folks in charge of repetition, the lunatics obsessed
with deeds, or sense of humor, or the obscenity of all sold out

ETTORE B

è chi non torna, o simula di non tornare, che si rovina
con le proprie mani: immonde, immuni; ciondolante
una lungo il fianco, insulsa testuggine l'altra, munita
di fionda (e armi rinunciate alle caviglie). Poi rostri
grigi, retrattili, improvvisi: *e quanto fa di cilindrata*
codesto automobile — chiese il glottologo equiparante
al collega incline ai riti del sorpasso. — Cinquemila. —
Accidenti! — Ribatté il primo senza togliere gli occhi
da quel Pacifico in cui gli era parso di scorgere la fine
del sogno americano. È un gioiello, è *nu babbà*, la Ford
del '50, o del '40, o del '30; ma un modello può farsi
pernicioso se diventa necessario approfittarne, iniettarlo
per via muscolare come un olio canforato, spiegando
che il desiderio di uno provoca desiderio negli altri,
abitando nell'Altro il desiderio primario cui competono
le funzioni (secondaria e terziaria) dell'insegnamento
e della dettatura: "l'acquisto del senso tragico da parte
di genti meccaniche, confinate per secoli al romanzo,
è l'opposto dell'insabbiare, azione creata per ribadire
che non è accaduto quello che non sarebbe mai dovuto
accadere". Oggi, specialmente, che l'uomo si evolve da
burocrate a faccendiere. Per la resa dei conti non resta
che aspettare la volta buona, leggere, senza battere ciglio
il bollettino di guerra dettato da un dio che si estingue,
vulgato dai più ricamati tra i capitani di una fedelissima
(e inceppatissima) legione. Vince, nella corsa, chi elargisce,
una per una, le mele d'oro, o le arachidi della minaccia
e del sotterfugio. Perdere, perde solo chi cambia mestiere

ETTORE B

it's those who don't return or feign they haven't yet
returned who hurt themselves with their own two hands:
one immune and filthy hand, dangling along the side,
the other looking like a senseless turtle, set with a sling
(more discarded weapons at ankle's level). Then sudden,
gray, retracting rams: *how much horsepower does your*
car have? — asked the comparative linguist of his colleague
skilled in the daring art of overtaking vehicles. — Four
hundred and fifty — You don't say! replied the linguist staring
at the Pacific Ocean where he thought he'd caught a glimpse
of the last American dream. A gem, the cream of the crop
this model Ford from the '50s, or the '40s, or even the '30s,
but a model can be destructive if you are forced to take
advantage of it, to inject it intramuscularly as if it were
camphor oil, and explain that a desire surfacing in A
kindles the same in B, and in others. For it's the Other
that charges the primary urge with the task (secondary and
tertiary) of teaching and dictation: "when proletarians, confined
for centuries to fiction, acquire a taste for tragedy, all cover-ups
are exposed, all ploys to repeat that what was not supposed
to happen didn't happen in fact, especially in these times of ours
when men are evolving from bureaucrats to fixers". To settle
scores all you can do is wait for the right moment, reading, without
batting an eyelash, the bulletin of war scribbled by a fleeting god
and echoed by the most decorated generals of the most trustworthy
(and most screwed up) legionnaires. It is who hands out the golden
apples, one at a time, or the peanuts of threat and subterfuge, that
wins the race. Losers are those who keep switching jobs

HANS D

se non torna chi è nudo in mezzo a nudi osceni, e non comporta,
la sua nudità, profezie primaverili, orientamenti, se non è iscritto
alla lega, e non si arrende al disgelo universale, all'imboscata
ipocrita che dilava i manoscritti e i coppi, le ringhiere, gli scoli
bercianti "tutti a casa" (*ma ti, lumaghin, cascia foeura i to cornin*
che doman l'è San Martin), il goal del pareggio anche stavolta
lo segna, inesauribile, Badoglio: *di là dal mar ci sta i camin che*
fumano: saranno la mia morosa che si consumano, o saranno
preludio di un mondo dove non dura che un'ora l'impareggiabile
zigzag di una farfalla, mentre una collega grassa e stronza ti arriva
magari a novant'anni. Lo segna perché non si dica che sono stati
solo i tedeschi ad avvilirvi, a sprofondarvi nelle sabbie mobili
di un esito che non vi riguardava, di cui non facevate veramente
parte. Oh ma quanto più spudorato questo suo goal-abbandono,
questo uno a uno, quanto più *jamme jamme*, più *pommadora*, più
ih che bellezza! Così, se non torna, o torna postumo, il sedotto da
una voglia di farsi avanti, conterà ugualmente come guadagno,
se non illecito almeno inatteso, come romanzo famigliare tràdito
da una voce che si stravolge nel ritmo ipercalorico di una cambiale
protestata: *tedaroonbi / cerdevin / tedaroonbi / cerdesgnappa*

HANS D

if those who don't return are naked among the naked and the obscene,
if their nudity doesn't stir up springtime prophecies and orientations, if
they are not members of the league and won't surrender to universal
thaw, the hypocrite ambush that washes away manuscripts and roof tiles,
handrails and drains that bellow "everybody go home" (*push out, your
tiny horns, my teeny weeny snail, for tomorrow is St. Martin's day*), then
it is Badoglio (again!) who scores the tying goal: *Those smoking chimneys
across the sea: it must be my true love they're burning.* Or could it be the
prelude to a world where the zigzag of a butterfly beyond compare may last
a day, an hour, while that fat asshole of your colleague might make it to
ninety years? He scores so that Germans alone could not be blamed to have
sunken you in the punishing quicksand of an outcome that was no concern
of yours, of which you wanted no part. And how shameful to score by merely
neglecting, by leaving behind! How despicably clownish his sullen and self-
righteous *hurry, hurry up,* his *more tomato sauce,* and *ah what a beauty!*
That way if they do not come back, or do so posthumously, those who
simply cannot resist the temptation of elbowing their way to the top, will
count their gain all the same, if not illicit, unforeseen, like a family romance
halted by the voice that twists in the hyper-caloric rhythm of a protested bill
of exchange: *Illgiveyouagla / ssofwine / Illgiveyouagla/ ssofschnapps*

ma qui più del pari, è l'andata in vantaggio che conta,
con un goal che distingue l'uomo dalla bestia (e dalla
iena in particolare), e proprio allo scadere del primo
tempo. Cento, mille, diecimila anime in pena, ignare
del delirio tumultuoso che le schiaccia come, tra due
parentesi, una disdascalia (*sottovoce, guardandosi
negli occhi, smascellarsi*), segnano abbandonate dal
più elementare degli istinti, e mosse soltanto da quella
pulsione che piuttosto che niente si attacca al concetto
(tutto incluso) di patria: «Ferito una prima volta alle
gambe [come già Garibaldi], rifiutava ogni soccorso
e rimaneva sul posto. Colpito una seconda volta da una
bomba di mortaio al petto e al viso che lo rendeva quasi
cieco [la sintassi, spiace dirlo, non è degna dei tempi],
persisteva nella lotta. Raggiunto una terza e ultima volta
dal piombo avversario, in piedi, proteso verso il nemico
(in fuga?), cadeva, al grido di "Viva l'Italia", convinto
che una cosa sola, decisiva spesso, trascinatrice sempre,
supremamente vale: l'esempio». Ma più che alla
lettera del sospettoso enunciato, meglio sarebbe stato
ispirarsi al biglietto di una lotteria sparagnina per cui
una dozzina di salme ricomposte sulle rive di un mare
(di un Piave?) senza osteria, decretò che l'essere altrove
fosse la nuova legge, l'insipido tornaconto e la summa
di tutti gli slogans secondo i quali i paredri sono uguali
alle sirene dei padri (o di chi ne fa le veci), e ai padri
confessori. A una bolgia più nera discendono i preposti
alla *res publica*, alle ruffianate: gli smemorati siete voi,
le più alte cariche che non seppero intendere, e tuttavia
non intendono, né il senso di quella strage, né quello del
grande spettacolo dei burattini in cui l'hanno precipitata

ETTORE B

here, of course, more than tying, what matters is being
ahead by the goal separating man from beasts (hyenas
in particular), and doing so just before the end of the first
half. Unaware of the delirious rage that crushed them like
a caption between two brackets (*sotto voce, staring into
one another's eyes, sides splitting with laughter*), a hundred,
a thousand, ten thousand grieving souls forsook the most
primal of their instincts, and scored, moved only by the drive
that, failing all else, clings to the concept (all inclusive) of
fatherland: "First wounded in his legs [like Garibaldi in his
own days], he turned down all help and held his post.
Struck a second time by a mortal shell in the chest and face,
and rendered nearly blind [the syntax, sadly, doesn't quite
fit the occasion], he did not surrender. Struck a third and
final time by adversarial fire, he stood up against a whole
host of enemies and fell to the cry of 'long live Italy,'
knowing that one thing only, often decisive, always
driving, reigns supreme: to be of example". But rather than
by the literalness of a dubious report, it may be wiser to draw
inspiration from a tight-fisted lotto ticket whereby half a dozen
corpses recomposed along the bank of a sea (of a Piave
bereft of taverns?) decreed that being elsewhere was the
new law, the tasteless advantage and the sum of all slogans
in which minor gods equate the sirens that were our fathers,
or their substitutes, or their father confessors. To a darker pit
of hell will fall those who held the reins of the *res publica*,
and their own dirty dealings: yes they are the ones who have
taken leave of their wits, the highest offices of the State who
neither then nor now could fathom the sense of a massacre
they have dealt with, for so long, as it were a puppet show

VOCI ANONIME
NEGLI SPOGLIATOI

ieri ho ricevuto due lettere, e l'ultima era in data 25
7 cioè il giorno prima che eventi di grande importanza
avvenissero in Italia. Sono però fiducioso che tutto ciò
non abbia per nulla intralciato il tuo progetto, e che
mentre io ti scrivo tu sia già a ***, per goderti un po'
di quel meritato riposo che tu meriti… Mi fa piacere
sentirmi dire… e ti garantisco che non vedo l'ora…
poterlo ancora prendere in braccio e rivederlo con
i miei occhi. Ma anche quel giorno dovrà venire, Dio
non potrà disporre altrimenti, sarebbe troppo brutto
negarmi di riabbracciare i miei cari, almeno per una
volta sola. Ma è meglio che cambi discorso altrimenti
scendo in una china che potrebbe rattristarti, mentre
io desidero che tu ti mantenga quella che ho in mente
io e così al nostro riavvicinamento non ci sarà da dire
nulla di questo tempo perduto, ma faremo come se
non ci fossimo mai lasciati. O mia cara, vorrò amarti
fino a stancarti, e tu perdonerai queste mie prepotenze
……………………………………………………………………..
……………………………………………………………………..
ce n'è che strisciano, che scavano, che si contorcono,
che dicono d'essere matti da legare, che non fanno
più parte del progetto di adeguare il mondo all'idea,
ma c'è più odore di bruciato che di non sapere; ce n'è
che insistono a parlare di denaro inviato; e ce n'è anche
che dicono noi no, noi eravamo con voi. Ma, gli uni
e gli altri si contano ormai sulle dita di mani annerite,
oleose, cadute per via da un carro di assiomi putrefatti

ANONYMOUS VOICES
FROM THE LOCKER ROOMS

Yesterday I got two letters. The second dated 7/25, the day
before events of great significance took place in Italy. I'm quite
confident though, that none of this got in the way of your project,
and that as I am writing, you are already at ***, relishing the well-
earned rest that you deserve... I like to hear you tell me... and rest
assured that I can hardly wait... could I only take him in my arms
again, and see him with my own two eyes. That day must come as
well, and God cannot arrange things otherwise. It would be too
cruel if I were denied the chance to embrace my loved ones again,
just once. But I better change the subject or I'll go down a path
that might sadden you, when I want you to stay the way I've
always known you, so when we meet, there won't be any talk of
lost time and we'll act as if we'd never parted. Darling, I want to
love you until I wear you out, if you'll forgive my boldness

. . . .
. . . .

There are some who crawl, who dig, who squirm, who say they're
raving mad, no longer part of this plan to adapt the world to
the idea, but the smell of burning is stronger than the smell of not
knowing. And there are some who insist on talking about the money
they sent home. And even some who say, not us, we've always
been on your side. But all of them can now be counted on the fingers
of blackened, oily hands, falling off a wagon of putrefied axioms

HANS D

impercettibile *auditu*, da quasi sessanta anni dura
il tempo della ripresa, una buriana di mancamenti,
di superfici ammaccate da discorsi atrabiliari e una
pioggia, un presuntuoso palleggio d'idiozie di cui
due finite in porta meritatamente (nessun reclamo
da parte dei tedeschi: gente che i figli a scuola li ha
sempre mandati, e all'estero, quand'era necessario).
Fu Taviani a segnare, per l'Italia, nel cinquantasei,
su passaggio di Martino. Quasi un Hitchcock, questo
Taviani (ma meno *hitch* che *cock*, a parlargli), tentò
di dire *scordammoce 'o passato*, ignaro che piange
di continuo il banco del cancellato, e con violenza
ritorna, e prende senso e dolore solo che lo si lasci
durare cancellato. Quasi una pera matura (ma più
che pera, un ananas, ad ascoltarlo), questo Taviani,
che tura per occultare (ma non dura) i buchi della
storia e protegge da giudizio avvilente la serratura
della *Wehrmacht*, che la Nato nuovamente la reclama
garante della pace, quella pace inusitata che nessun
Arbeit aveva saputo garantire. E io lo vedo dalla mia
finestra enfatica come siano avvolti nel sudario del
capitale quelli che dicono ma buttati tu nel fuoco
che a me basta un canovaccio senza trama, fatto
di cartapesta, privo di virtù proiettiva, un modesto
turbamento che una pioggerellina di marzo ci mette
un momento a portarselo via: c'è ancora chi nega
che il *boom* della Fiat fosse meglio del bum bum
non dei cannoni, ma dei missili (imperfettissimi)
di quei morti di fame dei russi? Da cui discende il
il terzo abbandono, segnato per conto di chi era
morto senza capire che sarebbe ancora inutilmente
morto, e rimorto, o in croce, o sparato alle spalle

HANS D

hear ye, hear ye all, the second half went on some sixty
unending years: a squall of swooning, of surfaces battered
by bilious words and sudden bursts of rain, a haughty ball-
drill of idiocies, two of which scored fair and square (no
complaints from the Germans: folks who never failed to
send their kids to public school, and abroad if necessary).
It was Signor Taviani who scored, for Italy, in 1956, on a
pass from his teammate Martino. A sort of Hitchcock, this
Taviani (more *cock* than *hitch*, however, when you talk to
him) who tried to say *forget the past,* unaware that the
removed is an ante that constantly weeps, and comes
back with a vengeance, and grows in sense and pain for
as long as it remains removed. A sort of ripe pear (more
than a pear, a pineapple, to hear him say things), this
Taviani fellow, bent on plugging up the gaps of history
(but it won't work) and thus erase a vilifying judgment from
the high forehead of the *Wehrmacht,* in which NATO saw
a guarantee of peace, that unsuspected peace no *Arbeit* could
ever guarantee. And I can see from my emphatic window
 just how wrapped up in the shroud of *Das Kapital* are those
who say why don't *you* go through fire and water; a plot-
less scenario is good enough for me, made of papier-mâché,
devoid of all projective virtues, rippled at most by a slight
disturbance any March drizzle can wash away in the blinking
of an eye. Is there still someone who denies that a booming
season at FIAT is far superior to the ludicrous banging out
not merely of cannons, but of the most primitive rockets hastily
assembled by Russian schlemiels? This is how the third goal
happened to be scored, on behalf of all those forsaken troops
who died without a shred of knowledge, without the slightest
suspicion they had died and would die for no good rime or
reason, over and over again, on the cross … or shot in the back

ETTORE B

ci vogliono prove ulteriori? Ma più prove di così... la stola,
la coda, il volpino, i mobili di teak, che da quando è mondo
il mondo non si era... Quanto al *cupio dissolvi*, al cupamente
introiettato, se la vedano i tifosi, i camerati, i radioascoltatori,
in ascolto. Quanto al *mazziare* che segue le corna (al segnare
per estremo abbandono di buon senso), chi meglio di Ciampi
(condannato a tirare di scherma da solo) avrebbe saputo dire:
i mali antichi li curi la vergogna? Ecco un caso esemplare
di *faciteme 'o ppiacere*, cui ribatte la domanda se non sia
piuttosto la coscienza del suo zero, del suo non sapersi mai
disporre ad altro, l'essenza del dramma che regola i conti
grigioverdi di quella morte, come anche di questo orizzonte
d'inerzia. Si può fare, non rida (*con bonomia*), caro ed illustre
(*con sarcasmo*) signor presidente; basterebbe non sbraitare
a favore di morti che non la riconoscono, e arginare l'infinita
sicumera di vivi (con licenza parlando) che sono adesso causa,
per quei morti, di strisciare ancora, alibi che svuota il senso
del loro inconfessato smarrimento. Quanto al tempo che lima,
ma non diluisce la scommessa di una storia che sputa sangue
ma non denuncia sopruso, è vero che ogni abuso comporta
un corpo ridotto a zero dal suo travestimento, da quel lattemiele
di che vuoi? cosa ti debbo dire? che ne fanno il sintomo
quieto, interlineare di un'usura ideale, di un ribrezzo. Accolga
quindi la nostra gratitudine: che chi alla tenera moglie aveva
preferito il turgido nuoto nei flutti gelidi del Reno e la maschia
lotta nel circo... e comunque ci aveva fottuto, cantando insieme
a noialtri, *noi soldaaa*, per merito suo è stato battuto quattro
reti a una (da lamento e desiderio di lamento, a morte
inimitabile, a cannocchiale con porno-zoom, a tiro al piccione)

ETTORE B

is more evidence necessary? Well, more than ... the stole,
the tail, the baby fox, the teak wood furniture that since the
Earth was born has never been... as to the *cupio dissolvi*
and its dismal interjections, let the fans, the comrades, the
radio-listeners decide. As to the insult added to injury (scoring
once more by ignoring every ounce of common sense), who
better than Signor Ciampi (doomed to fencing on his own)
would know how to say: let shame heal ancient evils? A perfect
case of *gimme a break*: the hiding of a crucial question. Might
not the awareness of his destitute and dour inability to envision
otherness, be the very essence of a tragedy that settled the gray-
green accounts of death, the way it does this inertial horizon?
It can be done, don't laugh (*all in good humor*), dear and rare
[*sic*] Mr. President: it would suffice not to holler in favor of dead
souls who do not acknowledge you, and stem instead the arrogance
of the living (so to speak) who now cause those dead to crawl
again and again and again, providing the alibi that robs the issue
of their tacit dismay. As for the time that files away without
decreasing the wager of a blood-spitting history (by which no
tyranny has yet been seriously compromised) is it not true that all
abuse involves a body brought to level zero by its own mask, by the
whipped cream of *che vuoi? what can I tell you?* morphing into the
quiet symptom of an ideal usury or repulsion? So, please, accept
our gratitude, for those who, over their tender wives, preferred a
turgid swim in the freezing waves of the Rhine, or a fight like real
men in the Circus... and screwed us anyhow, singing beside us *we
the soooldiers*) were beaten, thanks to you, four goals to one (from
moan to death beyond compare, to porno-zoom, to pigeon shooting)

CORO

chi organizza la propria vita ed è un ritorno la vita che organizza,
a lui gli tocca entrare in ogni fuga, restare con un pugno di mosche

chi trasferisce (negando) l'attesa di padre in figlio e si sgomenta
nel figlio, può fingersi maschio abbattuto in un campo di stoppie

chi per tutta la vita ritorna, ed è godimento in lui lo struggimento
del non tornare, la sua vita è lo stesso che passare da esasperato

senso a suono che suscita un riso: se basti, per ridere, occultare
il varco per cui si accede al gioco delle parti, alla ridda del tenere

a bada (fatto di gomma come sono, se gioco, gioco in porta, dove
anche i paranoici hanno diritto di sentirsi minacciati). Nel cretto

impassibile del segno (per cui si vince) che più si sdipana e più
minaccioso dimora, il Duce ha sempre ragione, sempre, i tedeschi,

torto. *Latine loquitur? Ufun pofocofo. . .* insomma me la cavo,
ma è chiaro che non c'è rimedio a ciò che si acquista fuggendo

CHORUS

he who crafts his life, and crafts it as a game of returns,
must take part in every breakaway, and end up with a fistful

of flies, he who, in denial, dismayed by his own son, transfers
expectations from father to son, can feign to be a male slain

in a field of stubble, he who spends his life retuning and finds
delight in the yearning of not returning, his life is the same as

passing from exasperated sense to sounds inducing laughter:
will it do, for laughter, to hide the gap that leads to a game of roles,

to the hassle of holding back? (As I am made of rubber, when I play,
I play goalie, where even paranoids can feel rightfully threatened.) In

the impassibly dry lakebed of the sign (by which you win) where threats
grow thicker the more they unravel, the Duce's always right, always the

Germans wrong. *Latine loqueris? Ittlelay itbay...* at the end of the day,
I get by, but clearly there is no cure against things acquired in retreat

A HISTORICAL NOTE ON CEPHALONIA 1943 – 2001

Cephalonia 1943-2001 is a narrative poem in the form of a dialogue or rather, a two-voiced monologue: a fragmented epic, contextualizing the massacre of Italian soldiers perpetrated by German troops in the days following the armistice, signed between Italy and the Allied Forces on September 8, 1943.

The voices belong to Ettore B, an Italian soldier fallen in combat, but possibly executed, and Hans D, a German businessman born with a silver spoon in his mouth, that is a man who always lands on his feet, before, during and above all after the war. Each character maintains a radically different relationship to the events. Ettore B's connection is real, raw and final. Hans D's is unmistakably surreptitious. Their role in these pages is clearly symbolic: the former is a victim. The latter, an indirect executioner. As such, Hans D faces the charge of being an inherent part of a culture based on contempt.

Not only on contempt, but on envy as well, as it is the case inevitably when despised human beings prove, practically against their own will, to be greater heroes than their own persecutors—those who believed they were the embodiment of absolute truth and, consequently, of tragic values. A baffling situation: thousands of disheveled, unshaven Alberto Sordi-like characters from the First and Second World Wars tragically redeem their wretchedly comic legacy and pass it on to countless enemies, wearing their impeccable military or bourgeois uniform. Having realized that their presumptuousness couldn't hold up, the party put to shame reacts with fury, feigning a badly disguised sense of superiority.

Under such circumstances, the Golden Apple of Discord is inscribed not to the fairest, but to the most tragic. The conflict and its consequences are staged in a willfully incongruous manner: the pseudo radiobroadcast of a soccer match, "overflowing" with commentary, but, as luck would have it, liberated from statistics. Here *agony* and *agon* are compatible signifiers, capable of a single deixis. In the horrifying match between Italy and Germany, which began in September of 1943 and lasted until March of 2001, Italy wins 4-1 (first half 2-1). A better score than in the 1970 Mexico City match (4-3) and even more memorable than the 1982 Madrid match (3-1).

To fully appreciate the tenor of the metaphor, we must shed some light on the adequacy of its vehicle: goals are instances of betrayal and abandonment, engendered by the shameful irresponsibility of people who believed then, and even now believe, that hiding their intellectual and emotional paucity behind a discourse of strategies (actually of stratagems), that have little to do with humanity is a legitimate way of proceeding. The victims of the greater number of betrayals and abandonments carry the day.

The second Italian goal must be counted as anomalous however. The soldiers of the Acqui Division "abandoned themselves", choosing to fight against an enemy that was bound to destroy them. When no rational explanation for an act implying suicide can be found in the language of those who performed it, or in the words ineptly attributed to them, it may be rewarding to search elsewhere. In the dark corner of hypotheses that contradict official reports and deter us from foolishly accepting explanations absurdly fabricated by mentally indolent, if not totally blind witnesses.

The Italian soldiers at Cephalonia accepted their fatal destiny. This fact alone should elicit some curiosity among those who still wish to speak about it, or at least hope to discover the presence of a death drive in the folds of the events. This would at least take away the bitter cup of nonsense with which professional politicians fill their mouths whenever they appoint themselves spokesmen for human suffering. The *raison d'état* they unhappily cling onto is nothing but the practice of a law allowing them to evaluate their own symptoms (and comforting delirium) as opportunities to have the world match their own sentiments of it, sooner or later.

No cause for alarm however: none of the rationalizations endlessly issued by these presumptuous hypnotizers of consciousness will ever capture the historical, testimonial and regenerative sense still lurking in the material reality of the events which they seem to stare at so intensely. To make this happen, words must collide and seduce each other, attract and rub against one another, stimulated by a powerful emotion and a genuine thirst for truth. Thus, the pseudo-catharsis stumbled on by the superficial authority of the guardians of the rules, paralyzed by habit, is challenged by the modest proposal of a poetic discourse in which *to name* and *to refer* are experienced not as a symbolic confirmation of reality, but as opportunities, as openings... as long, reasoned and unreasoned plunges into the sea, of the unconscious perhaps... but never of unawareness.

L.B.

NOTES

p. 9. *the fallen and the shot, in those....:* "...the rain wouldn't cease to beat" is drawn from the verses of Angiolo Silvio Novaro. They are imprinted in the minds of all Italian scholars and schoolchildren alike. "What does the drizzle of March tell us, when it beats, silvery... ...on the fig and mulberry tree..."

p. 11. *the double joint of a will that awakens....:* "To cut furrows with a plow and to defend it with the sword." A fascist slogan written on walls during World War II.

p. 11. *wear the little stars we wear...:* From a popular tune sung by soldiers: *E le stellette che noi portiamo...* – *And the little stars* [star shaped buttons] *we wear...*

p. 13. *while it rains and pours...:* From Ada Negri's *Rami di pesco — Peach Blossoms*: "While rain pours down between gusts of wind... / a little old woman sells peach blossoms."

P. 15. *alighting on hills...:* From the chorus of *Nabucco*, words by Temistocle Solera, and music by Giuseppe Verdi.

p. 17. *by the disbelief...:* "that we had taken up arms and fought to kill them, like that" Inspired by Mario Monicelli, who in his legendary *La grande guerra* entrusts almost the exact words to the great Alberto Sordi in the final scene of the film: "Ma che s'ammazza la gente così? - How do you like it? Killing people like that..." See also note p. 79.

p. 21. *that enables them also...* deprived of the letter *S* the Latin verb *noscere* (to know) becomes phonetically akin to *nocere* (to do harm). As everyone knows, unsurpassable harm is done when the letter *S* is doubled.

p. 25. *offered you by those...:* Benito Mussolini, on November 19th, 1941, announced to the *gerarchi* of the regime "I argued five years ago that we will crush the Negus's kidneys. Now, with the same absolute certainty, I repeat absolute, I am telling you that we will crush the kidneys of Greece in two to twelve months... ...the war has just begun!"

p. 25. *of founts and altars, and. . .:* The Lingotto is a district of Turin and the location of the building that once housed FIAT automobile factory.

p. 26. *to cling onto some. . .Oh, how beautiful the lovely land where sì resounds . . .* Approximately from Dante's *Inferno*, XXXIII, 80.

p. 26. *like a jig-saw-puzzle?. . .: The paintbrush* of the original text (pennello) has been turned into a *jig-saw puzzle* to preserve the play on words.

p. 29. *insatiable: quis talia fando. . .:* Virgil, *Aeneid*, Book II -- "What Myrmidon, or Dolopian, or warrior of fierce Ulysses, could hold back tears in telling such a story?"

p. 31. *compartments, impervious to explosion. . .:* The closing words ("the sea would close above us") from Dante's *Inferno*, XXIV, 142.

p. 33. *from the style one bids farewell to it. . .:* In Shakespeare's *Macbeth*, the fact that "nothing in his life became him like the leaving it" is said of Cawdor in Act I, Scene IV. The haunting words are pronounced by Malcolm.

p. 35. *better with: "Your Majesty, I. . .:* Echo of a phrase Mussolini pronounced before King Vittorio Emanuele III, upon meeting with him after the March on Rome.

p. 35. *the froth of all the* Porte Romane. . .: "with young girls in flower. . ." From the Milanese song *Porta Romana bella*, "And there are young girls that first wish you Good night and then (euphemistically) shake your hand. . ."

p. 35. *a surreptitious proxy; pretend a shrub. . .:* Inspired by Paul Celan's *Cenotaph, From Threshold to Threshold*.

p. 35. *unscathed sandstone, tragedy welcomes. . .:* Gray-green (grigioverde) had been the color of the uniform of the Italian Army since December 1908.

p. 37. *possible intellect) that clearly absolves. . .:* "No one beloved etc.": a verse from Dante's *Inferno*, V, 103.

p. 37. *of a father on horseback riding. . .:* From Victor Hugo's *Après la bataille (After the Battle.)* ". . .My father, moved, handed to his faithful hussar a canteen of rum that hung from his saddle. . ." ". . .aimed at my father's forehead crying 'Caramba!'. . ."

p. 37. *like a teratologist....:* The last words of this verse would have a familiar ring to anyone who remembers Italy in the 1960s, from the famous radio and TV advertising slogan for a powder detergent: "You can't get it any whiter, even with bleach!"

p. 39. *fill in for a fungus, then barrel down....:* An impossible play on words: *fungere da fungo,* — to function as a mushroom.

p. 45. *more evasive and scattered than men....:* "Lay a rug etc." Here is an almost word by word description of a skit performed by George Robey, English music hall comedian and singer, as reported by Emilio Cecchi in his *Pesci rossi* (first published in 1940).

p. 45. *the nightmare that the urns....:* Echoes Ugo Foscolo's *I sepolcri,* line 151.

p. 47. *under the whistling wind and....:* A mixture of lines from Giovanni Pascoli's *Lavandare* (Washerwomen) and *Fischia il vento* (The Wind Blows), a very popular song whose text was written in September 1943, at the inception of the Civil War. The music is that of the famous Russian song *Katyusha.* Along with *Bella ciao* it is one of the most famous songs celebrating the Italian Resistance.

p. 57. *goes all the way to* Ronchetto....: Ronchetto delle rane (Ronchetto of the frogs,) *Campazzo* (the bad meadow,) and *Ca' de la paura* (House of fear) are localities in the southern outskirts of Milan.

p. 59. *and the bewildered newsman....:* Irritated with reporters, the notorious secretary and socialist Prime Minister Bettino Craxi blurted out to one of them "vaffaonbagn" (literally go take a bath). The expression, very common in Lombardy, is a euphemism for ("go screw yourself") and was misunderstood by a puzzled correspondent for the *New York Times* who proposed it to his readers as yet another example of Italy's political extravagance.

p. 59. pive nel sacco *whose essence....:* To be left with "flutes (or bagpipes) in the bag" means, literally, to be disappointed as well as to be left empty-handed.

p. 59. *afar, but rather hopelessly losing....:* "The rice etc." The closing words refer to the Chinese ideogram for "thought" that is formed by the combination of two distinct pictograms: one representing the heart (above) and one representing a rice field (below).

p. 61. *never show, or those who squeeze. . .:* In a soccer match, a "sudden death" occurs when two teams are tied at the end of the game and overtime is required. The match ends as soon as one of the two teams scores the first goal.

p. 63 *decay of* do ut des. *Abandoned. . .:* "Bad dog leo" is a mock British pronunciation of the infamous name Pietro Badoglio, pronounced bə-ˈdōl yō ˈ.

p. 67. *of exchange:* Illgiveyouagla. . . .: An oddly clustered string of Lombard words. When reconstructed back into separate words, it reads as *"I'll give you a glass of wine / I'll give you a glass of schnapps.* It's also a continuation of the earlier verse, "push forth your tiny little horns. . ." referring to a curious event called Festa dei Cornuti (The feast of cuckolds), held in honor of St. Martin, bishop of Tours and patron saint of all those who have ever been cheated on by their partners.

p. 69. *corpses recomposed along the. . .: of a Piave* etc. Echoes a popular alpine song from World War I. "Di qua, di là del Piave / ci sta un'osteria. / Là c'è da bere /e da mangiare / ed un buon letto da riposar." "On both sides of the river Piave there was a tavern. . . There you could always find something good to eat and drink. . . and a warm bed to sleep in. . ."

p. 79. *values. A baffling situation. . .:* Alberto Sordi (1920–2003), one of Italy's greatest, most treasured cinematic stars best known for his parodies of the national character and social mores. See also note p. 17.

Rail Editions would like to thank the Dedalus Foundation for the permission to reproduce Robert Motherwell's *Black Gesture* series.

List of Plates

Robert Motherwell, *Black Gesture*, 1975. Acrylic on paper, 26 x 20 1/2 inches (66 x 52.1 cm), irreg. Courtesy of the Dedalus Foundation, © Dedalus Foundation, Inc./Licensed by VAGA, New York, NY.

Robert Motherwell, *Hanging Gesture*, 1975. Acrylic on paper, 20 x 22 1/2 inches (50.8 x 57.2 cm), irreg. Courtesy of the Dedalus Foundation, © Dedalus Foundation, Inc./Licensed by VAGA, New York, NY.

Robert Motherwell, *Black Gesture*, 1975. Acrylic on paper, 22 1/2 x 20 inches (57.2 x 50.8 cm), irreg. Courtesy of the Dedalus Foundation, © Dedalus Foundation, Inc./Licensed by VAGA, New York, NY.

Robert Motherwell, *[Untitled (Black Shape)]*, 1975. Acrylic on paper, 20 x 22 1/2 inches (50.8 x 57.2 cm), irreg. Courtesy of the Dedalus Foundation, © Dedalus Foundation, Inc./Licensed by VAGA, New York, NY.

Robert Motherwell, *Black Gesture*, 1975. Acrylic on paper, 26 x 20 1/2 inches (66 x 52.1 cm), irreg. Courtesy of the Dedalus Foundation, © Dedalus Foundation, Inc./Licensed by VAGA, New York, NY.

Robert Motherwell, *Black Gesture*, 1975. Acrylic on paper, 20 x 22 1/2 inches (50.8 x 56.5 cm), irreg. Courtesy of the Dedalus Foundation, © Dedalus Foundation, Inc./Licensed by VAGA, New York, NY.

Robert Motherwell, *[Untitled (Black Shape)]*, 1975. Acrylic on paper, 20 1/2 x 26 inches (52.1 x 66 cm), irreg. Courtesy of the Dedalus Foundation, © Dedalus Foundation, Inc./Licensed by VAGA, New York, NY.

Robert Motherwell, *Black Gesture*, 1975. Acrylic on paper, 20 x 22 1/2 inches (50.8 x 56.5 cm), irreg. Courtesy of the Dedalus Foundation, © Dedalus Foundation, Inc./Licensed by VAGA, New York, NY.

Luigi Ballerini was born in 1940, and lives in New York and Milan. He has taught Modern and Contemporary Italian Literature at New York University (1984-1990) and the University of California at Los Angeles (1991-2010). The author of numerous essays on Italian Futurism, avant-garde literature and poetry, medieval poetry, historical gastronomy, and contemporary sculpture, he has also edited several bilingual anthologies of Italian and American poetry and translated into Italian a variety of American authors ranging from Melville to William Carlos Williams and Gertrude Stein. His poetry has appeared under the following titles: *eccetera. E* (1972), *Che figurato muore* (1988), *Che oror l'orient* (1991), *Il terzo gode* (1994, *The Cadence of a Neighboring Tribe*, English edition, 1997) *Stracci shakespeariani* (1996), *Uscita senza strada* (2000), *Uno monta la luna* (2001), *Cefalonia* (2005, 2013), *Se il tempo è matto* (Mondadori, 2010), *Una dozzina + 3*, (2012). A Spanish language edition of *Cefalonia* was published in 2013. A volume of his collected poems (1972-2015) will be published by Mondadori in April 2016.

Charles H. Traub, 2015. Courtesy the artist.